CULTURE, GLOBALIZATION AND THE WORLD-SYSTEM

CULTURE, GLOBALIZATION AND THE WORLD-SYSTEM

CONTEMPORARY CONDITIONS FOR THE REPRESENTATION OF IDENTITY

Edited by
ANTHONY D. KING

University of Minnesota Press
Minneapolis

Published by the University of Minnesota Press
111 Third Avenue South, Suite 290
Minneapolis, MN 55401-2520
http://www.upress.umn.edu

Third printing 2000

Printed in the United States of America on acid-free paper

Library of Congress Cataloging-in-Publication Data

Culture, globalization, and the world-system : contemporary
    conditions for the representation of identity / edited by
    Anthony D. King.
        p.   cm.
    Papers presented at a symposium held at the State University of
New York at Binghamton on April 1, 1989.
    Originally published: Binghamton : Dept. of Art and Art History,
State University of New York at Binghamton, 1991. With new pref.
    Includes bibliographical references and indexes.
    ISBN 0-8166-2953-6 (pb)
    1. Culture—Congresses.   2. Acculturation—Congresses.
3. Ethnicity—Congresses.   I. King, Anthony D.
GN357.C848   1997
306—dc21   97-2347

Contents

CONTENTS

Preface to the
Revised Edition

SINCE THE ESSAYS IN THIS BOOK WERE FIRST PRESENTED AT AN INTER-
national symposium in upstate New York in 1989, there has been a phe-
nomenal growth of interest in the subject of globalization. Yet, relatively
little of the literature on this topic has addressed the many complex
questions arising from the impact of globalization on specifically cultural issues or, indeed, of culture(s) on the processes of globalization,
however those two very problematic concepts are interpreted.[1] If this is
one good reason for bringing out a second North American edition of
this book, another is the continued relevance of the many powerful arguments and different perspectives raised by its various contributors.
Encouraged, therefore, by the positive reception accorded the first edition, the enthusiastic support of editor Micah Kleit at the University of
Minnesota Press, and, in a more pragmatic sense, the somewhat furtive
circulation of its predecessor,[2] I start this preface to the revised edition.

As I indicated in the original edition, each term of the main title is associated with the name of particular leading scholars — the authors of the
principal papers here — who, over the past two decades, have pioneered

---

[1] In addition to the titles cited here, *Public Culture* (1988-), the journal of the Society for
Transnational Cultural Studies, and *Theory, Culture and Society* (1983-) provide valuable
guides to the existing literature.

[2] Published under the imprint of my parent department, the title never quite made it
into the American edition of *Books in Print*. Outside North America, the book is published
by Macmillan (London) and, in Japanese, by Tamagawa University Press.

the study of issues that the title suggests, some focusing primarily on questions of culture, others on the world political economy, still others on questions of societal transformation and identity formation. Yet, despite their different positions and different conceptual languages, all share, to a greater or lesser extent, at least two perspectives: the rejection of the nationally constituted society as the appropriate object of discourse, or unit of social and cultural analysis, and in different ways and to varying degrees, a commitment to conceptualizing "the world as a whole."

Since the book was first published, these authors, either on their own or in collaboration with others, have continued to forge ahead, developing their ideas and, in some cases, responding to issues and questions raised at the 1989 symposium, stimulating our thoughts and extending our vision.[3] In addition, a growing number of authors have both interrogated and reinterpreted notions of globalization and the world-system, or, as I later suggest, have responded by refusing them. Other scholars have pursued some of the more focused issues they prompt: the future of national identities and cultures; the rethinking of ideas of modernity, religion, and world history from a perspective of globalization; the localization of the global; the transformation of state-centric assumptions in the social sciences; and, in the humanities, ways of theorizing contemporary novels as examples of the globalization of culture.[4] These and many other studies of globalization, in widely different fields, are surely indicative of a major paradigm shift taking place in the way that the scholarly production of knowledge is being

[3] For example, David Morley and Kuan-Hsing Chen, eds., *Stuart Hall: Critical Dialogues in Cultural Studies* (London and New York: Routledge, 1996); Ulf Hannerz, *Transnational Connections: Culture, People, Places* (London and New York: Routledge, 1996); Roland Robertson, *Globalization: Social Theory and Global Culture* (London, Newbury Park, and New Delhi: Sage, 1992); and Immanuel Wallerstein, *Geopolitics and Geoculture: Essays on the Changing World-System* (Cambridge: Cambridge University Press, 1991) and *After Liberalism* (New York: New Press, 1995). Both in this volume and in other publications, Robertson, as well as other scholars mentioned here, take up a number of the points made by Janet Wolff in her concluding critical essay; see note 4 and also essays in Morley and Chen, *Stuart Hall*; and Hannerz, *Transnational Connections*.

[4] Malcolm Waters, *Globalization* (London and New York: Routledge, 1995); Tony Spybey, *Globalization and World Society* (Cambridge: Polity, 1996); Anthony Giddens, *Modernity and Self-Identity: Self and Society in the Late Modern Age* (Cambridge: Polity, 1991); Frederick Buell, *National Culture and the New Global System* (Baltimore: Johns Hopkins University Press, 1994); Jonathan Friedman, *Cultural Identity and Global Process* (London, Thousand Oaks, and New Delhi: Sage, 1994); Mike Featherstone, Scott Lash, and Roland Robertson, eds., *Global Modernities* (London, Thousand Oaks, and New Delhi: Sage, 1995); Peter Beyer,

rethought at the close of the second millennium, a time in historical space when additional symbolic meaning is being invested in the construction of a new space in historical time. It is fair to predict that scholars in an increasing number of specialized fields, from architecture to zoology, not only will look to existing theories of "the world as a single place," to quote Roland Robertson, but also will, through their own fields of expertise and research, refine and develop them.

Illustrative of the emergence of more specialized studies in this area has been the increasing use of the notion of "global culture." In recently reviewing some twenty books and essays in which the term either figures in the title or is defined and discussed in the text,[5] I became aware of a number of points. First, perhaps, is the very obvious one that the word "global" has acquired a certain fashionable éclat, now used, without definition or explanation, where previously "worldwide," "universal," or "everywhere" would have sufficed. More seriously, however, Featherstone writes that as there is a wide variety of responses to the processes of globalization, there is "little prospect of a unified global culture, rather there are global cultures in the plural."[6] Yet, meanings accorded to "global culture" differ. Recognizing this, there is a temptation to suggest a basic distinction between what might, from a spatial perspective, be termed centripetal and centrifugal uses: in the first, cultural forms, influences, and practices from many parts of the world locating at a place or population are seen to create a new "global culture";[7]

Religion and Globalization (London, Thousand Oaks, and New Delhi: Sage, 1994); Bruce Mazlish and Ralph Buultjens, eds., Conceptualizing Global History (Boulder, Colo.: Westview, 1993); Rob Wilson and Wimal Dissanayake, eds., Global/Local: Cultural Production and the Transnational Imaginary (Durham, N.C.: Duke University Press, 1996); Peter J. Taylor, "On the Nation-State, the Global, and Social Science," Environment and Planning A, 28 (1996), with commentaries from fourteen social scientists currently writing on globalization; Michael Valdez Moses, The Novel and the Globalization of Culture (Oxford and New York: Oxford University Press, 1995).

[5] Anthony D. King, "The Problem of Global Culture and the Internationalization of Architecture," in Distanzierte Verstrickungen: Die ambivalente Bindung soziologisch Forschender an ihren Gegenstand. Festschrift für Peter R. Gleichmann, eds. Eva Barlösius, Elcin Kürsat-Ahlers, and Hans-Peter Waldhoff (Berlin: Sigma Verlag, forthcoming, in German). The following paragraphs draw from this.

[6] Mike Featherstone, "Global Culture: An Introduction," in Global Culture: Nationalism, Globalization and Modernity, ed. Featherstone (London, Newbury Park, and New Delhi: Sage, in association with Theory, Culture and Society, 1990), 8.

[7] For example, Karen Fog Olwig, Global Culture, Island Identity: Continuity and Change in the Afro-Caribbean Community of Nevis (Philadelphia: Harwood, 1993).

in the second (more commonly), cultural influences or practices, stemming from one location, are said to be found, in various forms, in many parts of the globe.[8] (Neither of these, incidentally, is a particularly new phenomenon.)

Such a dichotomy is all too simple, however. If there are globally produced cultures, there are (as Robertson maintains) culturally produced views of globality. Where John Dobson assumes the increasing existence of a global corporate culture,[9] the more widely held opinion is that specific cultural practices and institutions, when not resisted, are invariably indiginized,[10] hybridized,[11] subjected to processes of cultural translation in the manner of their reception. Globalization is not a one-way process, nor does it come from a single source. Furthermore, its effects are not equally distributed in a global situation of grossly uneven development.[12] Arjun Appadurai's idea of a variety of cultural flows, stemming from different social, spatial, and historical locations (see pages 10–11 of the Introduction), along with alternative interpretations,[13] still has value. More recently, the less-than-elegant "glocalization," a Japanese marketing neologism from the 1980s, has been proposed to capture the process whereby the global is adapted to differentiated local conditions.[14] There is, however, still a tendency in many studies to delineate, in relation to material, media, or professional cultures, a process of global *production* — legitimate in itself — yet to ignore the very different circumstances of their reception/consumption and the meanings invested in this process.[15]

---

[8] For example, Karla Poewe, ed., *Charismatic Christianity as a Global Culture* (Columbia: University of South Carolina Press, 1994); and other examples in Waters, *Globalization*, among others.

[9] John Dobson, "The Role of Ethics in Global Corporate Culture," *Journal of Business Ethics*, 9 (1990): 481–488.

[10] Gyan Prakash, "Science 'Gone Native' in Colonial India," *Representations*, 40 (Fall 1992): 153–178.

[11] Jan Nederveen Pieterse, "Globalization as Hybridization," in Featherstone, Lash, and Robertson, *Global Modernities*, 45–68.

[12] Anthony McGrew, "A Global Society?" in *Modernity and Its Futures*, eds. Stuart Hall, David Held, and Tony McGrew (Cambridge: Polity Press, 1992), 62–113.

[13] Waters, *Globalization*, 156–157.

[14] Roland Robertson, "Glocalization: Time-Space and Homogeneity-Heterogeneity," in Featherstone, Lash, and Robertson, *Global Modernities*, 25–44.

[15] We must also acknowledge that the increasing numbers of people in the category of global travelers are likely to be inclined to accord similar meanings to globalized phenomena and hence the growth of "globe-talk."

All of these interpretations might be said to be "internal" to the notion of the global, encompassed within its boundaries, so to speak. At quite a different level, Kenneth Surin writes that "a theory of culture is something that is produced or created no less than its putative object. . . . A theory of culture, in this case, global culture, is not about culture/global culture itself but about the concepts that culture generates. A theory of culture does not impinge directly on culture but on the concepts of culture. It is a part of the process by which every culture generates for itself its own 'thinkability' (and 'unthinkability')."[16]

Yet, all of these views stem from a particular Western episteme. Because all stress the importance of transnational forces, the practices of coding and decoding everyday practices that disrupt, disturb, and even deny the identity of the global are not revealed.[17] One realm of intellectual inquiry that aims to do this, namely, the more historically and politically grounded arguments of postcolonial criticism, though crucial to this topic, is too extensive to be treated here.[18] Moreover, contestations of these representations of globalization are also likely to be found in major world religions. This raises the very basic question of whether it is actually possible for different geographical, social, political, religious, and cultural constituencies to work with the same concepts. And as only some of the works cited here address the question of gender,[19] there is clearly an urgent need to remedy this.[20]

In my original preface I made reference to the necessity of thinking about globality through the arts, in contrast to the (mainly) social science perspectives of the authors here. Although a growing body of theoretical work on globalization and the arts is emerging, the real answer to this question is to be found rather in the contents and contexts of their actual performance and practice rather than in theory — much of it

---

[16] Kenneth Surin, "On Producing the Concept of a Global Culture," in *Nations, Identities, Cultures*, ed. V. Y. Mudimbe. Special issue of *South Atlantic Quarterly*, 94 (1995): 1179–1200.

[17] I am indebted to Abidin Kusno for this comment.

[18] Reference must be made, however, to Edward Said's *Culture and Imperialism* (London: Chatto and Windus, 1993).

[19] For example, Spybey, *Globalization and World Society*; Robertson, *Globalization*.

[20] See, for example, Doreen Massey, *Space, Place and Gender* (Cambridge: Polity, 1994). A preliminary bibliographic search suggests that feminist research and writing are primarily focused on global economic, social, and political *issues* (including, but not limited to, the condition of women, as well as peace, health, ecology, and so on) rather than more generalized studies of globalization.

generated through the very historically, geographically, and spatially specific sites of world and global cities,[21] increasingly significant political and cultural formations that, until now, have been conceptualized and researched more in economic than social and cultural terms.[22] It is the very specificity and originality of novels, music, dance, video, poetry, graphics, film, photography, theater arts, painting, architecture, radio, television, carnival arts, public sculpture, and their equally distinctive cultural politics and political effects, their personal and community histories and memories, that will help refine the next generation of theorizing about globalization in the political, social, and, especially, cultural sphere.

Anthony D. King
Binghamton, NY
September 1996

---

[21] Paul L. Knox and Peter J. Taylor, eds., *World Cities in a World-System* (Cambridge: Cambridge University Press, 1995); Anthony D. King, *Global Cities: Post-Imperialism and the Internationalisation of London* (London and New York: Routledge, 1990); Saskia Sassen, *The Global City: New York, London, Tokyo* (Princeton, N.J.: Princeton University Press, 1991); Sharon Zukin, *The Cultures of Cities* (Cambridge, Mass., and Oxford: Blackwell, 1995).

[22] For some initial consideration of the arts in this context see, for example, "The Global Issue: A Symposium," *Art in America*, 77 (July 1989); also Jean Fisher, *Global Visions: Towards a New Internationalism in the Visual Arts* (London: Kala Press, 1995), and selected papers in *Third Text* (1987–).

Acknowledgments

THE ESSAYS IN THIS COLLECTION WERE FIRST PRESENTED AT A ONE-day symposium held at the State University of New York at Binghamton in April 1989 and subsequently revised and edited for publication. The first two talks, by Stuart Hall, were given two weeks before the main symposium; the chapters that appear here represent slightly edited versions of the transcriptions made from the taped presentations. The symposium was supported by grants from the offices of the Dean, Vice-President and Vice-Provost for Graduate Studies and Research at the university. I would like to thank them and also many others who helped organize and make the conference possible, including the speakers; the associate dean of Harpur College, Trudy Cobb Denard; Steve Ross and Barbara Abou-El-Haj for chairing; Carol Breckenridge, editor of *Public Culture*; the Art History Graduate Students Union, particularly, its then president, Joe Socki; my art history colleagues, particularly John Tagg, Wendy Botting, and others who assisted in various ways; the members of the Fernand Braudel Center, especially Donna De Voist; George McKee for his advice; Mario A. Di Cesare for his help with the production of the first edition; Carol Marcy and Joan Scott of the Department of Art History; and especially the staff of the then University Manuscript Center, Lisa Fegley-Schmidt, Phyllis Antos, Lois Orzel, and Elizabeth Regan, for their excellent cooperation and expertise. Finally, my thanks to Abidin Kusno and Janet Wolff for their comments on the preface to this second edition.

Introduction:
Spaces of Culture,
Spaces of Knowledge

ANTHONY KING

I WANT TO START THIS INTRODUCTION BY LOOKING AT THE THREE terms used in the main title of this book and by explaining why they have been put together, if somewhat uneasily, to form one single idea.

Culture, whether in its material or symbolic form, is an attribute which people(s) are said to have; globalization is a process and the world-system is a structure. Each term is a construct associated, both in this book and more generally, with a substantial though distinct body of scholarship and also, with the names of individual scholars, modes of inquiry and academic disciplines.

I shall not attempt here to provide much elaboration of the term culture which, especially in recent years, has undergone yet more transformations of meaning. In the announcement of the symposium which formed the basis of this volume, reference was made to cultures as "socially organized systems of meaning expressed in particular forms" and to "the historical and sociological study of concrete cultural forms and practices." As Janet Wolff points out in her concluding chapter, however, the principal papers here operate both with different and, in some cases, undifferentiated notions of culture: the various authors use the term to refer, at different times, to ways of life, the arts and media, political or religious culture and attitudes to globalization. Both here and elsewhere, Immanuel Wallerstein differentiates between culture (usage I) as "the set of characteristics which distinguish one group from another" and usage II, in the belles lettres sense, as "some set of phenomena which are different from (and 'higher' than) some other set of phenomena within any one group,"[1] an evaluative distinction which many would see as part of the cultural problematic. For the purposes of this introduction, I shall try and collapse this distinction between what in crude terms one might broadly call older "anthropological" notions of culture (i.e. ways of life, values, beliefs) and "humanistic" ones (arts and media) and adopt Wolff's conceptualisation: i.e. by suggesting that culture in its sense of art, literature, film, practices of representation of all kinds, both draws from and participates in the construction of culture as a way of life, as a system of values and beliefs which, in turn, affects culture as a creative, representational practice, we can bridge what is often a gap between these different meanings. In this sense, the study of culture has become the particular province of Cultural Studies.

As a mode of academic and intellectual inquiry, Cultural Studies is particularly associated with the establishment, in 1964, of the Centre for Contemporary Cultural Studies at the University of Birmingham, England, under the Directorship of Richard Hoggart, Professor of English Literature, and subsequently, Stuart Hall, Director between 1968 and 1979.[2] According to Hall,[3] Cultural Studies arose from a concern that major cultural transformations were taking place in society, not least in working class culture, yet none of the "traditional" disciplines were addressing them. The emergence of Cultural Studies in the 1960s was part of a crisis that was to undermine the humanities and social sciences and which also represented a politicization of academic work. Essentially theoretical in its orientation,

---

[1] Immanuel Wallerstein, "Culture as the Ideological Battleground of the Modern World-System," in *Global Culture. Nationalism, Globalization and Modernity*, ed. Mike Featherstone (London, Newbury Park and New Delhi: Sage, 1990):33.

[2] Stuart Hall, Dorothy Hobson, Andrew Lowe, Paul Willis, eds., *Culture, Media, Language*, Working Papers in Cultural Studies, 1972–9 (London: Hutchinson, 1987):7.

[3] This paragraph draws on comments made by Stuart Hall at a Round Table Seminar, Department of Art and Art History, SUNY-Binghamton, 13 March, 1989.

drawing on Marxism, semiotics, feminism and other discourses, Cultural Studies was not seen as a discipline, but "an area where different disciplines intersect in the study of the cultural aspects of society."[4] Subversive in intent, the field was consciously concerned with transforming the practice of producing knowledge, with issues of cultural politics, and with asking cultural and theoretical questions in relation to power.

Along with Cultural Studies' epistemological, methodological and theoretical concerns of the 1970s and 1980s which, as Stuart Hall's contribution demonstrates here, have constantly been transformed by new critical paradigms, much of the work of Cultural Studies was solidly grounded in historical studies of English society, the three paradigmatic and foundational texts usually being acknowledged as Richard Hoggart's *The Uses of Literacy* (1958), Raymond Williams' *Culture and Society* (1961) and E. P. Thompson's *The Making of the English Working Class* (1968).[5] Subsequent influential texts such as Paul Willis's *Learning to Labor* have also followed in the same geographical, social and class context.

The question arises, however, as to whether the nationally defined society is the most appropriate unit either for cultural or for social analysis. It is immediately apparent here that, in discussing globalization from the particular point of view of "Englishness," of English cultural identity, Stuart Hall is moving between, and occupying, at least four inter-related yet still identifiable cultural spaces which I will call those of post-imperialism (Britain), post-colonialism (Jamaica, Britain/England, the USA, and other post-colonial spaces elsewhere) and what he terms "global mass culture" and the "global post-modern." Whilst each of these cultural spaces may be seen, hypothetically, as sub-cultural parts of an equally hypothetical "global culture," or maybe just pieces of a larger jigsaw, not all of them would be useful for placing the identity of say, a Turkish migrant in Germany, the Vietnamese community in New York or, to change the example, the built environment of South Korean workers in the Gulf.

These are precisely the kind of issues which are anticipated by Janet Wolff in her conclusion: first, we need a theory of culture "at

---

[4] *Culture, Media, Language*, 7.

[5] Stuart Hall, "Cultural Studies and the Centre: Some Problematics and Problems," *Culture, Media, Language*, 16.

the level of the international" and second, in suggesting that cultural theory "has started to move away from its earlier, rather ethnocentric approach to investigate the global dimensions of cultural production and consumption," acknowledgement of the limited, culture-specific contexts in which earlier cultural theory paradigms operated.[6] If both these propositions are accepted, they also imply that, in addition to needing a "differentiated" notion of culture, as Wolff suggests, we also need a differentiated notion of "the international" and "the global." This, to return to my opening paragraph, is precisely the reason for juxtaposing the contributions of Wallerstein on the world-system and Robertson on globalization with a discourse on culture. These I shall refer to in more detail below.

Any theory of the international, or global, would need to recognise both the totally different presuppositions, as well as conceptualizations resulting from them, of both these terms: at their simplest, the whole historical problematic of the formation of nation-states, the proliferation in the nineteenth and especially twentieth century of the idea of the nation, nationalism and national cultures (a result, Robertson would maintain, of increased globality) and the distinctive historical, and unequal, conditions in which the notion of the "*international*" was constructed.[7] This topic has a literature which is far too extensive to quote. Similarly, concepts of the global and globalization, especially as they have been foregrounded in the last two decades, with their implied trans- or even a-nationality, their implicit concern with "humankind," "the earth," as well as a range of other issues, would require very careful unpacking.[8] In either case, little could be achieved towards constructing "a theory of culture at the level of the international" or "investigating the global dimensions of cultural production" without very specific historically, geographically

---

[6] Ulf Hannerz in his paper here also suggests that "what is required is an overall conceptualization of contemporary culture which incorporates a sense of the pervasiveness of globalization."

[7] See Anthony D. King, "Viewing the World as One: Urban History and the World-System," in *Urbanism, Colonialism and the World-Economy* (London and New York: Routledge, 1990):78.

[8] An early attempt is made in Roland Robertson and Frank Lechner, "Modernization, Globalization and the Problem of Culture in World-Systems Theory," *Theory, Culture and Society*, 2 (1985) 3:103–18. According to the *Oxford English Dictionary*, the term "globalization" had entered the vocabulary at the latest by 1962.

4

and sociologically informed conceptualizations of "the world as a whole" and, to somewhat caricature this process, the "international level" taking especial notice of the economic, political, cultural and nation-state elements in the development of the world order and the "global dimensions" possibly focusing on the cultural, spatial, technological, material and representational dimensions of the construction of globality.[9] In any event, such an investigation, by also taking in different representations of the world as a whole, or globality, from different social, spatial or cultural locations in the world, would require not only a history and sociology of knowledge but also an historical geography of such to give equal treatment to contesting representations of "the world as a whole." Some of these issues are addressed by Robertson in his paper here.

Whilst these may be seen as essentially theoretical concerns, it might be preferable to start by looking at much more specific questions of cultural identity and the historical conditions which have produced them. Here, I shall return to the subject of Cultural Studies, its distinct historical relation to the study of English working-class culture and of contemporary culture in the UK. In particular, as a contribution to developing a theory of culture at an international level, I shall try and map out some aspects of the geographical, historical and cultural specificity of post-colonialism as one distinctive prism through which some contemporary cultural phenomena can be approached.

The "English working class," neither economically, socially, culturally nor spatially, can be understood as an autonomous unit (irrespective of its connection to the larger "British" class structure); its constitution resulted from occupying a particular space in an international division of labor, the other parts of which were as essential to its existence as they (the English working class) were as essential to theirs. The system of course, as Hall points out, was the colonial empire, which was not only a political and economic, but also a social and cultural system: without the sugar plantation workers in

---

[9] The source of this concern was prompted by a study of "the production of a global culture" as represented by the near global diffusion of one particular item, and settlement type, in the built environment: see Anthony D. King, "The Global Production of Building Form," in *Urbanism, Colonialism and the World-Economy*, 100–29, and *The Bungalow: The Production of a Global Culture* (London and New York: Routledge and Kegan Paul, 1984).

the West Indies there could have been no trade union labor at the Thameside's Tate and Lyle refinery in London; without workers in the Cadbury's Cocoa plant in Birmingham, there would be no cash crop cocoa labor in West Africa.

The cultural system which was the outcome of this political and economic system is most obviously, and importantly, represented by language, but not only that: it includes a mass of variations of common institutions ranging from administrative and religious practices to architecture, from university curriculae to literature. And historically, it includes the United States which, for the present, still retains English as its official language. Without this post-colonial, transnational cultural system (and I am not implying that it is hegemonic) the contents of this book would not be written in (international) English.

The shortcomings of any academic paradigm, be it sociology or cultural studies, conceived on the basis of a "national society," can be illustrated by two examples. With a potentially exponential growth in international migration, with many cultures existing far from their places of origin and indeed, not necessarily for any length of time (vide migrants from Kuwait, South Africa, the Soviet Union), there is no "nationally grounded" theoretical paradigm which can adequately handle the epistemological situation. It is not just that, increasingly, many people have no roots; it's also that they have no soil. Culture is increasingly deterritorialized.

In the second place, a knowledge paradigm based primarily on a nationally organized society, or at least, without a larger transnational frame, can also not cope with cultural phenomena which, while clearly related to those of that society, nonetheless circulate in, outside and around it, in the case of the UK, in the USA, India, Nigeria, South Africa, Australia, Hong Kong and elsewhere in the "English speaking" ecumene. The rapidly expanding post-colonial discourse in English, though itself posing distinctive problems in regard to its origins and location of both theoretical and political reference, is ample illustration.[10] Edward Said makes a similar point:

---

[10] See, for example, Bill Ashcroft, Gareth Griffiths, Helen Tiffin, *The Empire Writes Back. Theory and Practice in Post-Colonial Literatures* (London and New York: Routledge, 1989); Trinh T. Minh-ha, *Women, Native, Other. Writing Postcoloniality and Feminism* (Bloomington: Indian University Press, 1989); Gayatri C. Spivak,

INTRODUCTION

One of the canonical topics of modern intellectual history has been the development of dominant discourses and disciplinary traditions in the main fields of scientific, social or cultural inquiry. Without any exceptions that I know of, the paradigms for this topic have been drawn from what is considered exclusively Western sources. Foucault's work is one instance of what I mean and, in another domain, is Raymond Williams'. I mention these two formidable scholars because in the main I am in almost total sympathy with their genealogical discoveries to which I am inestimably indebted. Yet for both of them the colonial experience is quite irrelevant...

Elsewhere in the same article Said writes:

there have been no full-scale critical studies of the relationship between modern Western imperialism and its culture, the occlusion of that deeply symbiotic relationship being a result of it. More particularly, the extraordinary dependence — formal and ideological — of the great French and English novel on the facts of empire has never been studied from a theoretical viewpoint.[11]

Without this recognition of the historical specificity of colonialism it is impossible properly to comprehend one, if not the central phenomenon of many contemporary cultures: race and racism. This is why the study of specifically colonial cultures is an essential pre-requisite for the study of many contemporary post-colonial and post-imperial ones.

The Post-Colonial Critic (London: Routledge, 1990) and issues of the journal, Inscriptions brought out by the Group for the Critical Study of Colonial Discourse and Center for Cultural Studies, University of California at Santa Cruz, particularly, Travelling Theories, Travelling Theorists, ed. James Clifford and Vivek Dhareshwar, 1989. The question of whether the "rediscovery" of colonialism, postcolonialism, postcoloniality and its relevant discourses in particular regions and institutions of the US in the late 1980s has more to do with the restructuring, through "diversity," of American national cultural identity rather than social and cultural movements in the immediate "post-colonial" societies of Africa or Asia themselves is a problem which still remains to be addressed. Both Lata Mani and James Clifford provide valuable insights into the role of locality in the production of cultural theory in Inscriptions, 5, 1989.

[11] Edward Said, "Intellectuals in the Post-Colonial World," Salamagundi, 70–71 (Spring-Summer 1986):44–64, 62, 59.

As has been pointed out elsewhere,[12] the first substantial encounter between (to use all terms defined by the center to describe its "Other") Europe and non-Europe, between what have been called "developed" and "developing" societies, between capitalist and pre-capitalist economies, between white and non-white, between people largely of one cultural and religious background and those of many other cultural and religious backgrounds, took place in what were to become the colonies, not the metropole; in the periphery, not the core; in non-Europe, not Europe, whichever conceptualisation we prefer. The first globally multi-racial, multi-cultural, multi-continental societies on any substantial scale were in the periphery, not the core. They were constructed under the very specific economic, political, social and cultural conditions of colonialism and they were largely, if not entirely, products of the specific social and spatial conditions of colonial cities. Only since the 1950s (and somewhat earlier in the United States) have such multi-racial, multi-cultural, multi-continental urban cultures existed in any substantial way in Europe.

Since the 1950s, different terms have been invented (almost entirely by "the West" to map, in Roland Robertson's terms, the global condition: First/Second/Third World, North/South, developed/underdeveloped/developing, core/periphery/semi-periphery, and so on. The First/Second/Third World categories were first applied, using Western economic and social indicators, to measure processes of "development" in different market and centrally-planned economies. Yet if this classification were reinterpreted to refer historically to those societies which, racially, ethnically, socially and culturally first approximated to what today are the culturally diverse, economically, socially and spatially polarised cities in the West but also, increasingly, major cities round the world, what is now the Third World would historically more accurately be labelled the First World, and the First World would become the Third. In other words, the culture, society and space of early twentieth century Calcutta or Singapore pre-figured the future in a much more accurate way than did that of London or New York. "Modernity" was not born in Paris but rather in Rio. With this interpretation, Euro-American paradigms of a so-called "Post-Modernism" have neither much meaning nor salience outside the narrow geographical confines of Euro-America where they developed.

---

[12] Anthony D. King, *Urbanism, Colonialism and the World-Economy*, 7.

8

The point is made more specifically in Featherstone's introduction to *Global Culture* (1990) where he speaks of "third cultures" developing to facilitate transcultural communication:[13] the "third culture" idea has already almost half a century of history behind it, grounded in ideas of Malinowski, though relating specifically to a "colonial third culture" situation.[14]

To conclude this section, therefore, it is clear that, in certain locations, and certain cultural contexts, even indeed for certain cultural actors and practices, the relevant cultural space to which the discourse belongs is not, certainly, the "national" society, the "international" society nor even the economically and politically neutral, technologically-transformed space of "the global" but a much more historically and culturally inscribed space of post-colonialism. Though dependent on the location, the actors and the institutions, it could also be post-imperialism which is characterised by quite a different distribution of power.[15]

Yet while post-colonialism and post-imperialism fill a fair amount of the space in a world-wide cultural system, like the red or blue ink which colored the "imperial" parts of old maps of the world, they do not by any means occupy all of it. And whilst I have been focusing specifically on the English-speaking post-colonial cultural ecumene, it is equally evident that there are also the French, Spanish, Portuguese, Dutch, Japanese to mention the more important. I now want to return once again to the question in my opening paragraph as to why these three ideas of my title were put together.

The World-System and Globalization

I have so far been addressing the problem of a Cultural Studies paradigm based, if not primarily on the notion of a nationally-consti-

---

[13] Mike Featherstone, "Global Culture: An Introduction," in *Global Culture*, ed. Mike Featherstone (London, Newbury Park, New Dehli: Sage, 1990):9.

[14] See Anthony D. King, *Colonial Urban Development. Culture, Social Power and Environment* (London and New York: Routledge, 1976) 58 et seq.

[15] See note 10 on the role of locality.

tuted society, at least on one inadequately related to a larger social and cultural system.

For Immanuel Wallerstein, "the only kind of social system is a world-system which we define quite simply as a unit with a single division of labor and multiple cultural systems. It follows logically that there can, however, be two varieties of such world systems, one with a common political system and one without. We designate these respectively as world empires and world economies."[16]

Yet just as Cultural Studies has represented its object without reference to the rest of the world (whether through the "world-system," the "international level" or "the global"), so the world-system perspective has represented the world, until relatively recently, without much reference to culture. One could therefore add to Wallerstein's formulation above that there could be two varieties of world-system, one with a common political (and, I would add, elements of a common social and cultural) system, especially as it is linked by language, cultural practices and institutions (i.e. the world-empires) and the second, without a common political (but, I would add, with strong elements of a social and cultural) system (i.e. the world economy). In the former, we might locate Hall's post-colonial and post-imperial discourse; in the latter, his propositions about a "global mass culture" and an "American conception of the world." The two, of course, are inter-related.

The extent to which one can begin to map out, and develop, even to the limited extent I have done here with colonial and post-colonial cultures, the conceptual language which would capture the culture of the capitalist world-economy is a task yet to be undertaken. One might refer, for example, to Appadurai's five dimensions of global cultural flows which move in non-isomorphic paths:

ethnoscapes produced by flows of people: tourists, immigrants, refugees, exiles and guest workers. Secondly, there are *techno-scapes*, the machinery and plant flows produced by multinational and national corporations and government agencies. Thirdly,

---

[16] Immanuel Wallerstein, "The Rise and Future Demise of the World Capitalist System: Concepts for Comparative Analysis," *Comparative Studies in Society and History*, 16 (1974):390; also in ibid. *The Capitalist World-Economy* (Cambridge University Press, 1979).

there are *finanscapes*, produced by the rapid flows of money in the currency markets and stock exchanges. Fourthly, there are *mediascapes*, the repertoire of images of information, the flows which are produced and distributed by newspapers, magazines, television and film. Fifthly, there are *ideoscapes*, linked to flows of images which are associated with state or counter-state movement ideologies which are comprised of elements of freedom, welfare, rights, etc.[17]

Linked to these we may add, simply, the *town* and *landscapes* which are produced by the global diffusion of information, images, professional cultures and sub-cultures and supported by international capital flows.[18] It is in the context of these non-isomorphic flows that we can now turn to the third term in my title, globalization.

Roland Robertson has spelt out his use of this term in a number of papers: "the crystallization of the entire world as a single place," the emergence of "the global-human condition" and "the consciousness of the globe as such."[19] On the face of it, the notion of globalization, in its very neutrality, would seem to have much in its favor. Etymologically, global does not carry as much cultural, religious, historical baggage with it as does the term world with its historically richer connotations of worldly, unworldly, this/next world etc. Linguistically, world (the historical etymology of which takes up four pages in the *Oxford English Dictionary* compared to a mere half page for globe) is most frequently used to refer to the whole of humankind, human society, the earth or a region of it; globe, however, has a more limited connotation, referring more specifically to the earth or terrestrial globe. It is also much easier to set out an array of grammatical terms (noun, adjective, verb, etc.) for the latter than the former, (i.e. globe, global, globally, globalize, globalization, globality, globe-wide)

---

[17] Arjun Appadurai, "Disjunction and Difference in the Global Cultural Economy," *Global Culture*, 295–310, as paraphrased by Featherstone, Introduction, 6–7.

[18] Anthony D. King, "Architecture, Capital and the Globalization of Culture," *Global Culture*, 397–411.

[19] Roland Robertson, "Globalization and Societal Modernization: A Note on Japan and Japanese Religion," *Sociological Analysis*, 47 (1987):35–43; ibid. "Globalization Theory and Civilizational Analysis," *Comparative Civilizations Review*, 17 (1987):20–30.

and though the same is indeed possible for the concept of the world-system, (i.e. world-system, world-systemic, world-systemically, etc.) it is clear that the concepts covered by these terms are obviously very different (for example, the notion of social movements being anti-systemic cannot properly be reproduced in the global vocabulary). Yet if defined in terms of "the process by which the world becomes a single place," globalization has also its ambiguities, irrespective of its silencing of economic, political or cultural parameters. Does it, for example, merely imply a state of inter-connectedness? Or does the inter-connectedness take a special form (as in an international division of labor)? Does it imply cultural homogenization, cultural synchronization or cultural proliferation? What does it say about the direction of cultural flows? Is it the interaction of the local and the global, with the emphasis on the former, or vice versa? Is it the synchronization of temporality? Whilst Robertson speaks to some of these issues, the questions demonstrate that, on a global scale, culture has to be thought spatially, politically, economically, socially and historically and also very specifically.

As both Barbara Abou-El-Haj and Janet Wolff point out in their comments, the language of the debate forces particular positions and pre-empts particular options. The over-generalising sweep of globalization submerges difference at the local, regional or national scale. Abu-Lughod suggests that instead of looking at processes from the top down (or from the center to the periphery) we might better see them from the bottom up. We might, in this context, speak rather of de-localization[20] and, following the arguments of both Hall and Robertson concerning the oppositional potential of globalization, also refer to re-localization, re-nationalization.

In any event, in terms of developing a theory of culture at an international or global level, it seems evident that, dependent on the sphere of cultural production under discussion, ideas from both the world-systems perspective as well as globalization theory can be operationalised. To speak only in terms of the production of space, in all of its urban, architectural and built form dimensions, this can — both in the present and historic past — be very effectively under-

---

[20] Jean Gottman, "What Are Cities Becoming the Centers Of? Sorting Out the Possibilities," in *Cities in a Global Society*, eds. Richard V. Knight and Gary Gappert (Newbury Park, London, Delhi: Sage, 1989):58–67, 61.

stood by reference to "a single division of labor with multiple cultural systems." And in regard to the same realm of cultural production, Robertson's array of global concepts can be equally effective in helping to explain, if only in a small, but growing sector of built environments round the world, the production of both homogeneity and of difference.[21] The question of whether such phenomena are *consumed* as homogenous or different, by people with a range of cultural identities, is of course a totally different issue. And whilst it is true, as Janet Wolff points out, that concepts such as "the West," "Third World/First World," "center/periphery" are ideologically imbued constructs produced in discourse, it is equally the case that such constructs are constantly mobilized and used as if they were real. Even the concept of culture itself, as used by anthropologists, was of course invented by European theorists to account for the collective articulations of human diversity.[22]

The papers

Having given some indication as to why these papers, and their authors, were brought together it would be abusing an editorial privilege if, in providing brief introductions to them, I were to iron out the very different positions and perspectives they represent. One of the many points which emerges from Janet Wolff's very comprehensive summing up is that, despite some agreements, the more general factor is the absence of common ground between them as well as the gap in connecting the title and subtitle of the volume. In the following comments, I shall merely set out what I see as some of their salient and valuable points.

---

[21] King, *Urbanism, Colonialism and the World-Economy*; ibid., *Global Culture*.

[22] James Clifford, *The Predicament of Culture* (Cambridge, Mass: Harvard University Press, 1988) 273; for a particularly powerful illustration of the political use of specific "ideologically imbued constructs produced in discourse" informing the writer's positionality, see Lata Mani's self-description as "a postcolonial Third World feminist working on India in the United States," in her "Multiple Mediations: Feminist Scholarship in the Age of Multinational Reception," *Inscriptions*, 5 (1989):1–24, 5. Mani's article also provides a useful source for the necessary differentiation of feminist perspectives mentioned in the concluding chapter by Janet Wolff, particularly the need to locate these perspectives in relation to a (larger) colonial discourse.

More perhaps than other contributors, Stuart Hall addresses both
the sub-title and title of the main theme mapping, in his first paper,
the way in which differing configurations of the global and the local
are producing and transforming different subject positions. In looking at globalization from the point of view of English culture, he
demonstrates not only how "Englishness" was formed in the context
of imperialism but how the colonised other was constituted as part of
English cultural identity. Yet where both Wallerstein and Hannerz
see the nation state as the main organizer and prism for constructing
cultural identity, Hall, for a variety of reasons, sees this relationship
between the state and identity eroding, "the old political and social
terrain of Englishness being broken up"; with this erosion comes a
reaction, a narrower and more dangerous definition of identity,
driven by racism. Particularly interesting are Hall's comments on the
"new forms of globalization" which have to do with new forms of
global mass culture but which nevertheless remain, in terms of technology, capital, advanced labor, centered in the West. Yet the other
characteristic of this global mass culture is its peculiar form of homogenization,

> ... enormously absorptive of things ... but the homogenization
> is never absolutely complete, and it does not work for complete-
> ness . . It is wanting to recognise and absorb those differences
> within the larger, over-arching framework of what is essentially
> an American conception of the world . . It does not attempt to
> obliterate (local capitals) but operates through them. It has to
> hold the framework of globalization in place and police that
> system: it stage manages independence within it, so to speak.

The logic of capital works through specificity: a new regime of difference produced by capital. Hall adamantly rejects the notion of
globalization as a non-contradictory space; it is always contested, and
is always with contradictions. Indeed, "the most profound cultural
revolution has come about as a consequence of the margins coming
into representation"; "marginality has become a powerful space."
    The power of Hall's analysis comes out especially in his second
paper where the notion of identity is theorised specifically in terms
of its political consequences: identity is "the guarantee of authenticity." The five great de-centerings of modern thought have ended the
old logic of identity: Marx, lodging the individual or collective subject always within historical practices; Freud, confronting the self

14

with "the great continent of the unconscious," making it "a fragile thing"; Saussure and linguistics pre-empting the process of enunciation; the relativisation of the Western episteme by the rise of other cultures; and finally, the displacement of the masculine gaze. These old collective identities of class, race, nation, of gender and the West no longer provide the codes of identity which they did in the past; existence in the modern world is much more characterised by "technologies of the self." It is in this context, that Hall discusses, with the immense power of personal experience, the development of "Black" as a historical and cultural category of identity, the emergence of Black consciousness in Jamaica in the 1970s, "the most profound cultural revolution in the Caribbean. Much greater than any political revolution they've ever had" and also in Britain. The central question is living identity through difference and recognizing that "any politics which attempts to organize people through their diversity of identifications, has to be a struggle which is conducted positionally ... the Gramscian notion of the war of position."

Roland Robertson also takes up some of these themes, if in a different theoretical language. In a globally compressed world with increasingly polyethnic, nationally constituted societies, the conditions "of and for the identification of individual and collective selves" become ever more complex. Drawing attention to the civilizational basis of identity construction, Robertson suggests that "culture" has become a globally authoritative paradigm for explaining difference, a means for locating "the Other." He poses this question in the interesting alternative positions of *relativism* on one hand, and *worldism* on the other, a strategy which, temporarily at least, has the effect of making culture disappear. Despite their quite different positions, Robertson would seem to agree with Hall, at least implicitly, that capitalism thrives on the celebration, and construction of difference.

For Robertson, any discussion of globalization needs to address four elemental points of reference — national societies, individuals, the world system of societies and humankind. Here, he draws attention to the way in which globalization has involved the institutional construction of the individual as well as, drawing on Geertz, the increasing construction of "foreignness" and the globewide establishment of "minorities." Equally suggestive are his comments on the substantive, self-reflexive utilisation of theoretical societal constructs in the development of Japanese society, and the notion that "societalism" — the commitment to the idea of the national society — is a crucial ingredient of the contemporary form of globalization. Robertson, incidentally, is the only contributor to mention that the major world religions are much older than national societies: the culture of particular societies resulting from their interactions with other societies in the global system.

For Immanuel Wallerstein, the nation-state is the central organizing unit of culture, and nationalism "the quintessential particularism." Increasingly, nation states resemble each other in their cultural forms. The notion that there could be a single world culture finds deep resistances, opposed by political chauvinisms and by multiple counter cultures. Culture, in Wallerstein's view, is essentially a reactive force: defining culture is a question of defining boundaries that are essentially political boundaries of oppression and of defense against oppression. The history of the world, rather than moving towards cultural homogenization, has demonstrated the opposite: a trend to cultural differentiation and cultural complexity. With these developments, each individual increasingly belongs to many cultures — an alternative way of saying perhaps, as Stuart Hall points out, that people have multiple cultural identities. Increasingly, one goes through life picking up identities. In this sense, identity construction is never finished.

In Wallerstein's view, the state through its monopoly of policies and resources will over time clearly create a national culture, even if it did not have one before. Where people see themselves belonging to a "world culture" this is essentially the culture of dominant groups, a view also made by Hall though in reference to globalizing theories as "the self-representation of the dominant particular." It is from the state that both cultural uniformity as well as cultural resistance stems: the powerful coopt cultural resistance either by commodifying it or accommodating it in a kind of cultural corruption. The present concern with culture, in the opinion of Wallerstein, follows from the decline in faith in the economic and political arenas as loci of social progress and individual salvation. "Culture" and "identity" are means to help them regain their bearing.

For Ulf Hannerz, writing subsequently to the paper included here, there is no doubt that "there is now a world culture. It is marked by an organization of diversity rather than the replication of uniformity. It is created through the increasing interconnectedness of varied local cultures, as well as through the development of cultures without a clear anchorage in one territory. These are all becoming sub-cultures within the wider whole."[23] In this paper, Hannerz sees the world as increasingly becoming a global ecumene of persistent cultural interaction and exchange though with asymmetry between the center and periphery, the relationship is one-sided. He also suggests, echoing comments earlier in this introduction, that the "First World" has been present in the consciousness of the "Third World" much longer than the "Third World" has been in the minds of the "First." As other speakers, Hannerz suggests there is a need for alternative, much more complex scenarios for the study of cultural homogenization and, as with the subsequent intervention from Janet Abu-Lughod, draws on concrete ethnographical research from West Africa to back up his abstractions.

Hannerz proposes four typical frameworks for examining cultural process, "organized as a flow of meanings, by way of meaningful forms, between people": the market, the state, form of life and movements. He shares with Wallerstein the belief in the state as a strong organizational cultural force, constructing subjects culturally as citizens. But whilst recognizing that global cultural flows are unpacked, dismantled and reassembled, Hannerz also sees, like Hall, the autonomy of cultural competence which exists at the local level. Nonetheless, as the local division of labor is drawn into that at the international level, some forms of life more than others are defined more in terms of cultural flows from the center, and some people more than others are more involved with metropolitan systems of meaning. With movements (the women's, environmental and peace), Hannerz's four scenarios offer a considerably more sophisticated way of thinking about globalization, echoing some of Appadurai's models mentioned earlier. With these frameworks, he asks how people are drawn into world cultures and how, through technology and people, cultures become separated from territories. Hannerz's attention to the spatial ordering of culture prompts important questions about the inherent social and spatial units through which culture is organized: ethnicity, race, gender and class on one side, and the neighborhood, city, region, nation and the world on the other. These are ideas worth further development.

The extent to which the state organizes culture, moreover, clearly

---

[23] Ulf Hannerz, "Cosmopolitans and Locals in World Culture," *Global Culture*, 237.

depends on material conditions. And as Abou-El-Haj points out in her commentary on the Hannerz paper, this is equally true whether in the core or periphery, with culture constantly being "corrupted" and reconstituted in both places. Global culture results from multi-dimensional cultural flows and obviously comes from a number of different cores or centers.[24] In this context, Hannerz suggests that it is likely that increasingly cultural differences are to be found within societies, not between them, a point that I take up, in relation to the cultures of so-called "world cities," in my own paper.

I shall not attempt to comment on the five brief interventions which follow the main papers, each of which raises both a number of substantial issues as well as, in some cases, basic questions about the premises and organization of the debate. Whilst these interventions have, for convenience, been gathered together in one chapter, it should be mentioned that Janet Abu-Lughod's response was particularly addressed to the papers of Robertson and Wallerstein and that of Barbara Abou-El-Haj to that of Hannerz. Maureen Turim, John Tagg and myself each addressed the theme of the symposium in the context of our specific subject fields of cinema, photography and urbanism.

Finally, in writing this introduction, I have made considerable use of comments from the concluding paper by Janet Wolff, drafted partly prior to and also during the symposium and briefly revised shortly afterwards. Where these comments closed the "Current Debates in Art History" symposium for 1989, I have extended it into 1990 in this introduction, not least by reference to recent publications. Janet Wolff poses some excellent and fundamental questions and also provides leads for further research. I would, however, have to disagree that the project of a dialogue between the different discourses represented by the title and the sub-title is premature, as she suggests. It has in fact taken place. It will be up to the readers, reviewers and others to see whether it provides a basis for the debate to be developed.

---

[24] See Carol Breckenridge, Preface, *Public Culture*, 1 (1988) 1.

1. The Local and the Global: Globalization and Ethnicity

STUART HALL

THE DEBATE ABOUT GLOBALIZATION AS A WORLD PROCESS, AND its consequences, has been going on now in a variety of different fields of intellectual work for some time. What I am going to try and do here is to map some of the shifting configurations of this question, of the local and the global, particularly in relation to culture and in relation to cultural politics. I am going to try to discover what is emerging and how different subject positions are being transformed or produced in the course of the unfolding of the new dialectics of global culture. I will sketch in this aspect towards the end of this first talk and develop it in the second when I shall address the question of new and old identities. The question of ethnicity spans the two talks.

I am going to look at this from what might be thought of as a very privileged corner of the process, or rather, an unprivileged corner, a declining corner, that is, from the United Kingdom, and particularly, England. Certainly from the perspective of any historical account of English culture, globalization is far from a new process. Indeed, it is almost impossible to think about the formation of English society, or of the United Kingdom and all the things that give it a kind of privileged place in the historical narratives of the world, outside of the processes that we identify with globalization.

So when we are talking about globalization in the present context, we are talking about some of the new forms, some of the new rhythms, some of the new impetuses in the globalizing process. For the moment, I do not want to define it more closely than that but I do want to suggest that it is located within a much longer history; we suffer increasingly from a process of historical amnesia in which we think that just because we are thinking about an idea it has only just started.

As an entity and national culture, the United Kingdom rose with, and is declining with, one of the eras, or epochs, of globalization: that era when the formation of the world market was dominated by the economies and cultures of powerful nation-states. It is that relationship between the formation and transformation of the world market and its domination by the economies of powerful nation-states which constituted the era within which the formation of English culture took its existing shape. Imperialism was the system by which the world was engulfed in and by this framework, and also through the intensification of world rivalries between imperial formations. In this period, culturally, one sees the construction of a distinct cultural identity which I want to call the identity of Englishness. If you ask what the formative conditions are for a national culture like this to aspire to, and then acquire, a world historical identity, they would have a great deal to do with a nation's position as a leading commercial world power; it has to do with its position of leadership in a highly international and industrializing world economy, and with the fact that this society and its centers have long been placed at the center of a web of global commitments.

But it is not my purpose to sketch that out. What I am trying to ask something about is, what is the nature of cultural identity which belongs with that particular historical moment? And I have to say that, in fact, it was defined as a strongly centered, highly exclusive and exclusivist form of cultural identity. Exactly when the transformation to Englishness took place is quite a long story. But one can see a certain point at which the particular forms of English identity feel that they can command, within their own discourses, the discourses of almost everybody else; not quite everybody, but almost everyone else at a certain moment in history.

Certainly, the colonized Other was constituted within the regimes of representation of such a metropolitan center. They were placed in their otherness, in their marginality, by the nature of the "English eye," the all-encompassing "English eye." The "English eye" sees

20

everything else but is not so good at recognizing that it is itself actually looking at something. It becomes coterminous with sight itself. It is, of course, a structured representation nevertheless and it is a cultural representation which is always binary. That is to say, it is strongly centered; knowing where it is, what it is, it places everything else. And the thing which is wonderful about English identity is that it didn't only place the colonized Other, it placed *everybody* else.

To be English is to know yourself in relation to the French, and the hot-blooded Mediterraneans, and the passionate, traumatized Russian soul. You go round the entire globe: when you know what everybody else is, then you are what they are not. Identity is always, in that sense, a structured representation which only achieves its positive through the narrow eye of the negative. It has to go through the eye of the needle of the other before it can construct itself. It produces a very Manichean set of opposites. When I speak about this way of being in the world, being English in the world, with a capital "E" as it were, it is grounded not only in a whole history, a whole set of histories, a whole set of economic relations, a whole set of cultural discourses, it is also profoundly grounded in certain forms of sexual identity. You cannot think of what the true-born Englishman is — I mean, could you imagine advancing into the liberties of a true-born English*woman*? It's unthinkable. It was not a phrase that was around. A free-born English person was clearly a free-born English *man*. And the fully buttoned-up, stiff upper lip, corseted notion of English masculinity is one of the ways in which this particular cultural identity was very firmly stitched into place. This kind of Englishness belongs to a certain historical moment in the unfolding of global processes. It is, in itself, a kind of ethnicity.

It has not been polite until the day before yesterday to call it this at all. One of the things which happens in England is the long discussion, which is just beginning, to try to convince the English that they are, after all, just another ethnic group. I mean a very interesting ethnic group, just hovering off the edge of Europe, with their own language, their own peculiar customs, their rituals, their myths. Like any other native peoples they have something which can be said in their favor, and of their long history. But ethnicity, in the sense that this is that which speaks itself as if it encompasses everything within its range is, after all, a very specific and peculiar form of ethnic identity. It is located in a place, in a specific history. It could not speak except out of a place, out of those histories. It is located in rela-tion to a whole set of notions about territory, about where is home and where is overseas, what is close to us and what is far away. It is mapped out in all the terms in which we can understand what eth-nicity is. It is, unfortunately, for a time, the ethnicity which places all the other ethnicities, but nevertheless, it is one in its own terms.

If you ask something about the nation for which this was the major representation and which could represent itself, culturally and ideo-logically, through the image of an English identity, or an English ethnicity, you will see, of course, what one always sees when one examines or opens up an ethnicity. It represents itself as perfectly natural: born an Englishman, always will be, condensed, homoge-nous, unitary. What is the point of an identity if it isn't one thing? That is why we keep hoping that identities will come our way because the rest of the world is so confusing: everything else is turn-ing, but identities ought to be some stable points of reference which were like that in the past, are now and ever shall be, still points in a turning world.

But of course, Englishness never was and never possibly could be that. It was not that either in relation to those societies with which it was deeply connected, both as a commercial and global political power overseas. And one of the best-kept secrets of the world is that it was not that in relation to its own territory either. It was only by dint of excluding or absorbing all the differences that constituted Englishness, the multitude of different regions, peoples, classes, genders that composed the people gathered together in the Act of Union, that Englishness could stand for everybody in the British Isles. It was always negotiated against difference. It always had to absorb all the differences of class, of region, of gender, in order to present itself as a homogenous entity. And that is something which we are only now beginning to see the true nature of, when we are beginning to come to the end of it. Because with the processes of globalization, that form of relationship between a national cultural identity and a nation-state is now beginning, at any rate in Britain, to disappear. And one suspects that it is not only there that it is begin-ning to disappear. That notion of a national formation, of a national economy, which could be represented through a national cultural identity, is under considerable pressure. I ought to try and identify very briefly what it is that is happening which makes that an untena-ble configuration to keep in place for very much longer.

First of all, in the British case, it results from a long process of economic decline. From being the leading economic power in the world, at the pinnacle of commercial and industrial development, the first industralizing nation, Britain then became simply one amongst other, better, stronger, competing, new industrializing nations. It is certainly no longer at the forefront, or at the cutting edge, of industrial and economic development.

The trend towards the greater internationalization of the economy, rooted in the multinational firm, built on the foundations of Fordist models of mass production, and mass consumption long outran some of the most important leading instances of this which one can find in the British economy. From the position of being in the forefront, Britain has increasingly fallen behind as the new regimes of accumulation, production, and consumption have created new leading nations in the global economy.

More recently, the capitalist crisis of the seventies has accelerated the opening up of new global markets, both commodity markets and financial markets, to which Britain has been required to harness itself if it were not to be left behind in the race. With the horrendous noise of deindustrialization, Britain is, under Thatcherism, trying to ground itself somewhere close to the leading edge of the new technologies which have linked production and markets in a new surge of international global capital. The deregulation of the City is simply one sign of the movement of the British economy and the British culture to enter the new epoch of financial capital. And new multinational production, the *new* new international division of labor, not only links backward sections of the third world to so-called advanced sections of the first world in a form of multinational production, but increasingly tries to reconstitute the backward sectors within its own society: those forms of contracting out, of franchising, which are beginning to create small dependent local economies which are linked into multinational production. All of these have broken up the economic, political and social terrain on which those earlier notions of Englishness prospered.

Those are things which one knows about. Those are the constituent elements of the process which is called globalization. I want to add some other things to them because I think we tend to think about globalization in too unitary a way. And you will see why I am going to insist on that point in a moment.

Something else which has been breaking up that older, unitary formation is certainly the enormous, continuing migrations of labor in the post-war world. There is a tremendous paradox here which I cannot help relishing myself; that in the very moment when finally Britain convinced itself it had to decolonize, it had to get rid of them, we all came back home. As they hauled down the flag, we got on the banana boat and sailed right into London. That is a terrible paradox because they had ruled the world for three hundred years and, at least, when they had made up their minds to climb out of that role, at least the others ought to have stayed out there in the rim, behaved themselves, gone somewhere else, or found some other client state. No, they had always said that this was really home, the streets were paved with gold and, bloody hell, we just came to check out whether that was so or not. And I am the product of that. I came right in. Someone said, "Why don't you live in Milton Keynes, where you work?" You have to live in London. If you come from the sticks, the colonial sticks, where you really want to live is right on Eros Statue in Piccadilly Circus. You don't want to go and live in someone else's metropolitan sticks. You want to go right to the center of the hub of the world. You might as well. You have been hearing about that ever since you were one month old. When I first got to England in 1951, I looked out and there were Wordsworth's daffodils. Of course, what else would you expect to find? That's what I knew about. That is what trees and flowers meant. I didn't know the names of the flowers I'd just left behind in Jamaica. One has also to remember that Englishness has not only been decentered by the the great dispersal of capital to Washington, Wall Street and Tokyo, but also by this enormous influx which is part of the cultural consequences of the labor migrations, the migrations of peoples, which go on at an accelerated pace in the modern world.

Another aspect of globalization comes from a quite different direction, from increasing international interdependence. This can be looked at in two quite different ways.

First, there is the growth of monetary and regional arrangements which link Britain into NATO, the Common Market and similar organizations. There is a growth of these regional, supranational organizations and connections which simply make it impossible, if it ever was, to try to conceive of what is going on in English society as if it only had an internal dynamic. And this is a very profound shift, a shift in the conceptions of sovereignty, and of the nation-state. It is a shift in the conception of what the English government can do,

24

what is in its control, transformations which it could bring about by its own efforts. These things increasingly are seen to be interdependent with the economies, cultures and polities of other societies.

Last but not least is the enormous impact of global ecological interdependence. When the ill winds of Chernobyl came our way, they did not pause at the frontier, produce their passports and say, "Can I rain on your territory now?" They just flowed on in and rained on Wales and on places which never knew where Chernobyl was. Recently, we have been enjoying some of the pleasures and anticipating some of the disasters of global warming. The sources and consequences are miles away. We could only begin to do something about it on the basis of some form of ecological consciousness which has to have, as its subject, something that is larger than the freeborn Englishman. The freeborn Englishman cannot do anything about the destruction of the rain forest in Brazil. And he hardly knows how to spell ozone.

So, something is escaping here from this older unit which was the lynchpin of globalization of an earlier phase; it is beginning to be eroded. We will come to look back at this era in terms of the importance of the erosion of the nation-state and the national identities which are associated with it.

The erosion of the nation-state, national economies and national cultural identities is a very complex and dangerous moment. Entities of power are dangerous when they are ascending and when they are declining and it is a moot point whether they are more dangerous in the second or the first moment. The first moment, they gobble up everybody and in the second moment they take everybody down with them. So when I say the decline or erosion of the nation-state, do not for a moment imagine that the nation-state is bowing off the stage of history. "I'm sorry, I was here for so long. I apologize for all the things that I did to you — nationalism, jingoism, ferocious warfare, racism. I apologize for all that. Can I go now?" It is not backing off like that. It goes into an even deeper trough of defensive exclusivism.

Consequently, at the very moment when the so-called material basis of the old English identity is disappearing over the horizon of the West and the East, Thatcherism brings Englishness into a more firm definition, a narrower but firmer definition than it ever had before. Now we are prepared to go to anywhere to defend it: to the South Seas, to the South Atlantic. If we cannot defend it in reality, we

25

will defend it in mime. What else can you call the Falklands episode? Living the past entirely through myth. Reliving the age of the dictators, not just as farce but as myth. Reliving the whole of that past through myth, a very defensive organization. We have never been so close to an embattled defensiveness of a narrow, national definition of Englishness, of cultural identity. And Thatcherism is grounded in that. When Thatcherism speaks, frequently asking the question, "Are you one of us?" Who is one of us? Well, the numbers of people who are not one of us would fill a book. Hardly anybody is one of us any longer. Northern Ireland is not one of us because they are bogged down in sectarian warfare. The Scots are not one of us because they did not vote for us. The Northeast and the Northwest are not one of us because they are manufacturing and declining and they have not jumped on to the enterprise culture; they are not on the bandwagon to the South in their heads. No Blacks are, of course, not quite. There may be one or two who are "honorary" but you cannot really be one of us. Women can only be in their traditional roles because if they get outside their traditional roles they are clearly beginning to edge to the margins.

The question is still asked in the expectation that it might have been answered with the same large confidence with which the English have always occupied their own identities. But it cannot be occupied in that way any longer. It is produced with enormous effort. Huge ideological work has to go on every day to produce this mouse which people can recognize as the English. You have to look at everything in order to produce it. You have to look at the curriculum, at the Englishness of English art, at what is truly English poetry, and you have to rescue that from all the other things that are not. Everywhere, the question of Englishness is in contention.

All I want to say about that is, that when the era of nation-states in globalization begins to decline, one can see a regression to a very defensive and highly dangerous form of national identity which is driven by a very aggressive form of racism.

That is something of the story of questions of ethnicity and identity in an older form of globalization. What Thatcherism and other European societies are trying to come to terms with is how to enter new forms of globalization.

The new forms of globalization are rather different from the ones I have just described. One of the things which happens when the nation-state begins to weaken, becoming less convincing and less

26

powerful, is that the response seems to go in two ways simultaneous-ly. It goes above the nation-state and it goes below it. It goes global and local in the same moment. Global and local are the two faces of the same movement from one epoch of globalization, the one which has been dominated by the nation-state, the national economies, the national cultural identities, to something new.

What is this new kind of globalization? The new kind of globaliza-tion is not English, it is American. In cultural terms, the new kind of globalization has to do with a new form of global mass culture, very different from that associated with English identity, and the cultural identities associated with the nation-state in an earlier phase. Global mass culture is dominated by the modern means of cultural produc-tion, dominated by the image which crosses and re-crosses linguistic frontiers much more rapidly and more easily, and which speaks across languages in a much more immediate way. It is dominated by all the ways in which the visual and graphic arts have entered direct-ly into the reconstitution of popular life, of entertainment and of leisure. It is dominated by television and by film, and by the image, imagery, and styles of mass advertising. Its epitomy is in all those forms of mass communication of which one might think of satellite television as the prime example. Not because it is the only example but because you could not understand satellite television without understanding its grounding in a particular advanced national econ-omy and culture and yet its whole purpose is precisely that it cannot be limited any longer by national boundaries.

We have just, in Britain, opened up the new satellite TV called "Sky Channel," owned by Rupert Murdoch. It sits just above the Channel. It speaks across to all the European societies at once and as it went up all the older models of communication in our society were being dismantled. The notion of the British Broadcasting Corporation, of a public service interest, is rendered anachronistic in a moment.

It is a very contradictory space because, at the same time as send-ing the satellite aloft, Thatcherism sends someone to watch the satel-lite. So Mrs. Thatcher has put into orbit Rupert Murdoch and the "Sky Channel" but also, a new Broadcasting Standards Committee to make sure that the satellite does not immediately communicate soft pornog-raphy to all of us after 11 o'clock when the children are in bed.

So this is not an uncontradictory phenomenon. One side of Thatch-erism, the respectable, traditional side, is watching the free market side. This is the bifurcated world that we live in but nevertheless, in terms of what is likely to carry the new international global mass culture back into the old nation-states, the national cultures of European societies, it is very much at the leading edge of the transmitters of the image. And as a consequence of the explosion of those new forms of cultural communication and cultural representation there has opened up a new field of visual representation itself.

It is this field which I am calling global mass culture. Global mass culture has a variety of different characteristics but I would identify two. One is that it remains centered in the West. That is to say, Western technology, the concentration of capital, the concentration of techniques, the concentration of advanced labor in the Western societies, and the stories and the imagery of Western societies: these remain the driving powerhouse of this global mass culture. In that sense, it is centered in the West and it always speaks English.

On the other hand, this particular form does not speak the Queen's English any longer. It speaks English as an international language which is quite a different thing. It speaks a variety of broken forms of English: English as it has been invaded, and as it has hegemonized a variety of other languages without being able to exclude them from it. It speaks Anglo-Japanese, Anglo-French, Anglo-German or Anglo-English indeed. It is a new form of international language, not quite the same old class-stratified, class-dominated, canonically-secured form of standard or traditional highbrow English. That is what I mean by "centered in the West." It is centered in the languages of the West but it is not centered in the same way.

The second most important characteristic of this form of global mass culture is its peculiar form of homogenization. It is a homogenizing form of cultural representation, enormously absorptive of things, as it were, but the homogenization is never absolutely complete, and it does not work for completeness. It is not attempting to produce little mini-versions of Englishness everywhere, or little versions of Americanness. It is wanting to recognize and absorb those differences within the larger, overarching framework of what is essentially an American conception of the world. That is to say, it is very powerfully located in the increasing and ongoing concentration of culture and other forms of capital. But it is now a form of capital which recognizes that it can only, to use a metaphor, rule through other local capitals, rule alongside and in partnership with other economic and political elites. It does not attempt to obliterate them; it operates through them. It has to hold the whole framework of glob-

28

alization in place and simultaneously police that system: it stage-manages independence within it, so to speak. You have to think about the relationship between the United States and Latin America to discover what I am talking about, how those forms which are different, which have their own specificity, can nevertheless be repenetrated, absorbed, reshaped, negotiated, without absolutely destroying what is specific and particular to them.

We used to think at an earlier stage, that if one could simply identify the logic of capital, that it would gradually engross everything in the world. It would translate everything in the world into a kind of replica of itself, everywhere; that all particularity would disappear; that capital in its onward, rationalizing march would not in the end care whether you were black, green or blue so long as you could sell your labor as a commodity. It would not care whether you were male or female, or a bit of both, provided it could deal with you in terms of the commodification of labor.

But the more we understand about the development of capital itself, the more we understand that that is only part of the story. That alongside that drive to commodify everything, which is certainly one part of its logic, is another critical part of its logic which works in and through specificity. Capital has always been quite concerned with the question of the gendered nature of labor power. It has never been able to obliterate the importance to itself of the gendered nature of labor power. It has always been able to work in and through the sexual division of labor in order to accomplish the commodification of labor. It has always been able to work between the different ethnically- and racially-inflected labor forces. So that notion of the overarching, ongoing, totally rationalizing, has been a very deceptive way of persuading ourselves of the totally integrative and all-absorbent capacities of capital itself.

As a consequence, we have lost sight of one of the most profound insights in Marx's *Capital* which is that capitalism only advances, as it were, on contradictory terrain. It is the contradictions which it has to overcome that produce its own forms of expansion. And that until one can see the nature of that contradictory terrain and precisely how particularity is engaged and how it is woven in, and how it presents its resistances, and how it is partly overcome, and how those overcomings then appear again, we will not understand it. That is much closer to how we ought to think about the so-called "logic of capital" in the advance of globalization itself.

Until we move away from the notion of this singular, unitary logic of capital which does not mind where it operates, we will not fully understand it. Can I refer to a number of things we have not been able to understand as a consequence of reading *Capital* that way? We have not been able to understand why anybody is still religious at the end of the twentieth century. It ought to have gone; that is one of the forms of particularity. We have not been able to understand why nationalism, an old form of particularism, is still around. All those particularisms ought by now to have been modernized out of existence. And yet what we find is that the most advanced forms of modern capital on a global scale are constantly splitting old societies into their advanced and their not so advanced sectors. Capital is constantly exploiting different forms of labor force, constantly moving between the sexual division of labor in order to accomplish its commodification of social life.

I think it is extremely important to see this more contradictory notion, this whole line of development which is leading to different phases of global expansion, because otherwise we do not understand the cultural terrain that is in front of us.

I have tried then to describe the new forms of global economic and cultural power which are apparently paradoxical: multi-national but de-centered. It is hard to understand but I think that is what we are moving into: not the unity of the singular corporate enterprise which tries to encapsulate the entire world within its confines, but much more decentralized and decentered forms of social and economic organization.

Not everywhere, by any means, but in some of the most advanced parts of the globalization process what one finds are new regimes of accumulation, much more flexible regimes founded not simply on the logics of mass production and of mass consumption but on new flexible accumulation strategies, on segmented markets, on post-Fordist styles of organization, on lifestyle and identify-specific forms of marketing, driven by the market, driven by just-in-time production, driven by the ability to address not the mass audience, or the mass consumer, but penetrating to the very specific smaller groups, to individuals, in its appeal.

From one point of view, you might say that this is just the old enemy in a new disguise and that actually is the question I am going to pose. Is this just the old enemy in a new disguise? Is this the ever-rolling march of the old form of commodification, the old form of globalization, fully in the keeping of capital, fully in the keeping of the West, which is simply able to absorb everybody else within its drive? Or is there something important about the fact that, at a certain point, globalization cannot proceed without learning to live with and working through difference?

If you look at one of the places to see this speaking itself, or beginning to represent itself, it is in the forms of modern advertising. If you look at these what you will see is that certain forms of modern advertising are still grounded on the exclusive, powerful, dominant, highly masculinist, old Fordist imagery, of a very exclusive set of identities. But side by side with them are the new exotics, and the most sophisticated thing is to be in the new exotica. To be at the leading edge of modern capitalism is to eat fifteen different cuisines in any one week, not to eat one. It is no longer important to have boiled beef and carrots and Yorkshire pudding every Sunday. Who needs that? Because if you are just jetting in from Tokyo, via Harare, you come in loaded, not with "how everything is the same" but how wonderful it is, that everything is different. In one trip around the world, in one weekend, you can see every wonder of the ancient world. You take it in as you go by, all in one, living with difference, wondering at pluralism, this concentrated, corporate, over-corporate, over-integrated, over-concentrated, and condensed form of economic power which lives culturally through difference and which is constantly teasing itself with the pleasures of the transgressive Other.

You see the difference from the earlier form of identity that I was describing: embattled Britain, in its corsetted form, rigidly tied to the Protestant Ethic. In England, for a very long time, certainly under Thatcherism, even now, you can only harness people to your project if you promise them a bad time. You can't promise them a good time. You promise them a good time later on. Good times will come. But you first of all have to go through a thousand hard winters for six months of pleasure. Indeed, the whole rhetoric of Thatcherism has been one which has constructed the past in exactly that way. That is what was wrong about the sixties and seventies. All that swinging, all that consumption, all that pleasurable stuff. You know, it always ends in a bad way. You always have to pay for it in the end.

Now, the regime I am talking about does not have this pleasure/pain economy built into it. It is pleasure endlessly. Pleasure to begin with, pleasure in the middle, pleasure at the end, nothing but pleasure: the proliferation of difference, questions of gender and sexuality.

31

It lives with the new man. It produced the new man before anyone was ever convinced he even existed. Advertising produced the image of the post-feminist man. Some of us cannot find him, but he is certainly there in the advertising. I do not know whether anybody is living with him currently but he's there, out there in the advertising.

In England it is these new forms of globalized power that are most sensitive to questions of feminism. It says, "Of course, there'll be women working with us. We must think about the question of creches. We must think about equal opportunities for Black people. Of course, everybody knows somebody of different skin. How boring it would be just to know people like us. We don't know people like us. We can go anywhere in the world and we have friends who are Japanese, you know. We were in East Africa last week and then we were on safari and we always go to the Caribbean, etc.?"

This is what I call the world of the global post-modern. Some parts of the modern globalization process are producing the global post-modern. The global post-modern is not a unitary regime because it is still in tension within itself with an older, embattled, more corporate, more unitary, more homogenous conception of its own identity. That struggle is being fought out within itself and you may not see it actually. If you don't see it, you ought to. Because you ought to be able to hear the way in which, in American society, in American culture, those two voices speak at one and the same time. The voice of infinite pleasurable consumption and what I call "the exotic cuisine" and, on the other hand, the voice of the moral majority, the more fundamental and traditional conservative ideas. They are not coming out of different places, they are coming out of the same place. It is the same balancing act which Thatcherism is trying to conduct by releasing Rupert Murdoch and Sir William Rees Mogg at one and the same time, in the hope that they will kind of hold on to one another. An old petite bourgeois morality will constrain the already deregulated Rupert Murdoch. Somehow, these two people are going to live in the same universe — together.

So, the notion of globalization as a non-contradictory, uncontested space in which everything is fully within the keeping of the institutions, so that they perfectly know where it is going, I simply do not believe. I think the story points to something else: that in order to maintain its global position, capital has had to negotiate and by negotiate I mean it had to incorporate and partly reflect the differences it was trying to overcome. It had to try to get hold of, and neutralize, to some degree, the differences. It is trying to constitute a world in which things are different. And that is the pleasure of it but the differences do not matter.

Now the question is: is this simply the final triumph, the closure of history by the West? Is globalization nothing but the triumph and closure of history by the West? Is this the final moment of a global post-modern where it now gets hold of everybody, of everything, where there is no difference which it cannot contain, no otherness it cannot speak, no marginality which it cannot take pleasure out of?

It's clear, of course, that when I speak about the exotic cuisine, they are not eating the exotic cuisine in Calcutta. They're eating it in Manhattan. So do not imagine this is evenly and equally spread throughout the world. I am talking about a process of profound unevenness. But I am nevertheless saying that we shouldn't resolve that question too quickly. It is just another face of the final triumph of the West. I know that position. I know it is very tempting. It is what I call ideological post-modernism: I can't see round the edge of it and so history must have just ended. That form of post-modernism I don't buy. It is what happens to ex-Marxist French intellectuals when they head for the desert.

But there is another reason why one should not see this form of globalization as simply unproblematic and uncontradictory, because I have been talking about what is happening within its own regimes, within its own discourses. I have not yet talked about what is happening outside it, what is happening at the margins. So, in the conclusion of this talk, I want to look at the process from the point of view, not of globalization, but of the local. I want to talk about two forms of globalization, still struggling with one another: an older, corporate, enclosed, increasingly defensive one which has to go back to nationalism and national cultural identity in a highly defensive way, and to try to build barriers around it before it is eroded. And then this other form of the global post-modern which is trying to live with, and at the same moment, overcome, sublate, get hold of, and incorporate difference.

What has been happening out there in the local? What about the people who did not go above the globalization but went underneath, to the local?

The return to the local is often a response to globalization. It is what people do when, in the face of a particular form of modernity which confronts them in the form of the globalization I have described, they opt out of that and say "I don't know anything about that any more. I can't control it. I know no politics which can get hold of it. It's too big. It's too inclusive. Everything is on its side. There are some terrains in between, little interstices, the smaller spaces within which I have to work." Though, of course, one has to see this always in terms of the relationship between unevenly-balanced discourses and regimes. But that is not all that we have to say about the local.

For it would be an extremely odd and peculiar history of this part of the twentieth century if we were not to say that the most profound cultural revolution has come about as a consequence of the margins coming into representation — in art, in painting, in film, in music, in literature, in the modern arts everywhere, in politics, and in social life generally. Our lives have been transformed by the struggle of the margins to come into representation. Not just to be placed by the regime of some other, or imperializing eye but to reclaim some form of representation for themselves.

Paradoxically in our world, marginality has become a powerful space. It is a space of weak power but it is a space of power, none-theless. In the contemporary arts, I would go so far as to say that, increasingly, anybody who cares for what is creatively emergent in the modern arts will find that it has something to do with the lan-guages of the margin.

The emergence of new subjects, new genders, new ethnicities, new regions, new communities, hitherto excluded from the major forms of cultural representation, unable to locate themselves except as de-centered or subaltern, have acquired through struggle, sometimes in very marginalized ways, the means to speak for themselves for the first time. And the discourses of power in our society, the discourses of the dominant regimes, have been certainly threatened by this de-centered cultural empowerment of the marginal and the local.

Just as I tried to talk about homogenization and absorption, and then plurality and diversity as characteristic of the new forms of the dominant cultural post-modern, so in the same way one can see forms of local opposition and resistance going through exactly the same moment.

Face to face with a culture, an economy and a set of histories which seem to be written or inscribed elsewhere, and which are so immense, transmitted from one continent to another with such extra-ordinary speed, the subjects of the local, of the margin, can only come into representation by, as it were, recovering their own hidden histories. They have to try to retell the story from the bottom up, instead of from the top down. And this moment has been of such profound significance in the post-war world that you could not describe the post-war world without it. You could not describe the movements of colonial nationalism without that moment when the unspoken discovered that they had a history which they could speak; they had languages other than the languages of the master, of the tribe. It is an enormous moment. The world begins to be decolonized at that moment. You could not understand the movements of modern feminism precisely without the recovery of the hidden histories.

These are the hidden histories of the majority that never got told. History without the majority inside it, history as a minority event. You could not discover, or try to discuss, the Black movements, civil rights movements, the movements of Black cultural politics in the modern world, without that notion of the rediscovery of where people came from, the return to some kind of roots, the speaking of a past which previously had no language. The attempt to snatch from the hidden histories another place to stand in, another place to speak from, and that moment is an extremely important moment. It is a moment which always tends to be overrun and to be marginalized by the dominant forces of globalization.

But do not misunderstand me. I am not talking about some ideal free space in which everybody says, "Come on in. Tell us what you think. I'm glad to hear from you." They did not say that. But those languages, those discourses, it has not been possible to silence in the last twenty years.

Those movements also have an extraordinarily complex history. Because at some time, in the histories of many of them over the last twenty years, they have become locked into counter-identities of their own. It is a respect for local roots which is brought to bear against the anonymous, impersonal world of the globalized forces which we do not understand. "I can't speak of the world but I can speak of my village. I can speak of my neighborhood, I can speak of my community." The face-to-face communities that are knowable, that are locatable, one can give them a place. One knows what the voices are. One knows what the faces are. The recreation, the reconstruction of imaginary, knowable places in the face of the global post-modern which has, as it were, destroyed the identities of specific places, absorbed them into this post-modern flux of diversity. So one under-

35

stands the moment when people reach for those groundings, as it were, and the reach for those groundings is what I call ethnicity.

Ethnicity is the necessary place or space from which people speak. It is a very important moment in the birth and development of all the local and marginal movements which have transformed the last twenty years, that moment of the rediscovery of their own ethnicities.

But just as, when one looks at the global post-modern, one sees that it can go in both an expansive and a defensive way, in the same sense one sees that the local, the marginal, can also go in two different ways. When the movements of the margins are so profoundly threatened by the global forces of postmodernity, they can themselves retreat into their own exclusivist and defensive enclaves. And at that point, local ethnicities become as dangerous as national ones. We have seen that happen: the refusal of modernity which takes the form of a return, a rediscovery of identity which constitutes a form of fundamentalism.

But that is not the only way in which the rediscovery of ethnicity has to go. Modern theories of enunciation always oblige us to recognize that enunciation comes from somewhere. It cannot be unplaced, it cannot be unpositioned, it is always positioned in a discourse. It is when a discourse forgets that it is placed that it tries to speak everybody else. It is exactly when Englishness is the world identity, to which everything else is only a small ethnicity. That is the moment when it mistakes itself as a universal language. But in fact, it comes from a place, out of a specific history, out of a specific set of power relationships. It speaks within a tradition. Discourse, in that sense, is always placed. So the moment of the rediscovery of a place, a past, of one's roots, of one's context, seems to me a necessary moment of enunciation. I do not think the margins could speak up without first grounding themselves somewhere.

But the problem is, do they have to be trapped in the place from which they begin to speak? Is it going to become another exclusive set of local identities? My answer to that is, probably, but not necessarily so. And in closing, I will tell you one little local example why I give that answer.

I was involved in a photographic exhibition which was organized in London by the Commonwealth Institute. The Commonwealth Institute had this idea; it got money from one of the very large, ex-colonial banks who were anxious to pay a little guilt money back to the societies which they had exploited for so long, and they said:

"We'll give a series of regional prizes in which we'll use photography; we know that everybody in these societies doesn't have access to photography but photography is a widespread medium. Lots of people have cameras; it reaches a much wider audience. And we'll ask the different societies that used to be linked together under the hegemonic definition of the Commonwealth to begin to represent their own lives, to begin to speak about their own communities, to tell us about the differences, the diversities of life in these different societies that used to be all threaded together by the domination of English imperialism. That's what the Commonwealth was, the harnessing of a hundred different histories within one singular history. The history of the Commonwealth." This was a notion of using the cultural medium of photography to explode that old unity and proliferate, to diversify, to see the images of life as people in the margins represented themselves photographically. The exhibition was judged in the far regions of the world where there are Commonwealth countries, and then was judged centrally. What was that exhibition like?

We found precisely what enormous access can be given to such peoples when the margins are empowered, in however small a way. Extraordinary stories, pictures, images of people looking at their own societies with the means of modern representation for the first time. Suddenly, the myth of unity, the unified identity of the Commonwealth, was simply exploded. Forty different peoples, with forty different histories, all located in a different way in relation to the uneven march of capital across the globe, harnessed at a certain point with the birth of the modern British Empire — all these things had been brought into one place and stamped with an overall identity. You will all be in one, contribute to one overall system. That is what the system was, the harnessing of these differences. And now, as that center begins to weaken, so the differences begin to pull away. That was an enormous moment of the empowering of difference and diversity. It is the moment of what I call the rediscovery of ethnicity, of people photographing their own homes, their own families, their own pieces of work.

We also discovered two other things. In our naivety, we thought that the moment of the rediscovery of ethnicity, in this sense, would be a rediscovery of what we called "the past," of people's roots. But the funny thing is that the past has not been sitting down there waiting to be discovered. The people from the Caribbean who went home [where is that, you know?] to photograph the past [where is that, you know?]: what explodes through the camera is twentieth-century Africa not seventeenth century Africa. The homeland is not waiting back there for the new ethnics to rediscover it. There is a past to be learned about, but the past is now seen, and has to be grasped as a history, as something that has to be told. It is narrated. It is grasped through memory. It is grasped through desire. It is grasped through reconstruction. It is not just a fact that has been waiting to ground our identities. What emerges from this is nothing like an uncomplicated, dehistoricised, undynamic, uncontradictory past. Nothing like that is the image which is caught in that moment of return.

But then the second, more extraordinary thing is that people want to speak right out of that most local moment — what do they want to talk about? Everywhere. They want to tell you about how they came from the smallest village in the deepest recesses of wherever and went straight by New York to London. They want to talk about what the metropolis, what the cosmopolitan world looks like to an ethnic. They were not prepared to come on as "ethnic artists." "I will show you my crafts, my skills; I will dress up, metaphorically in my traditions, I will speak my language for your edification." They had to locate themselves somewhere but they wanted to address problems which could no longer be contained within a narrow version of ethnicity. They did not want to go back and defend something which was ancient, which had stood still, which had refused the opening to new things. They wanted to speak right across those boundaries, and across those frontiers.

When I stopped talking about the global, I asked, is this the cleverest story the West has ever told or is this a more contradictory phenomenon? Now I ask exactly the opposite. Is the local just the little local exception, just what used to be called a blip in history? It will not register anywhere, it does not do anything, it is not very profound. It is just waiting to be incorporated, eaten up by the all-seeing eye of global capital as it advances across the terrain. Or is it also, itself, in an extremely contradictory state? It is also moving, historically being transformed, speaking across older and new languages. Think about the languages of modern contemporary music and try to ask, where are the traditional musics left that have never heard a modern musical transcription? Are there any musics left that have not heard some other music? All the most explosive modern musics are crossovers. The aesthetics of modern popular music is the aesthetics of the hybrid, the aesthetics of the crossover, the aesthetics of the diaspora, the aesthetics of creolization. It is the mix of musics which is exciting to a young person who comes right out of what Europe is pleased to think of as some ancient civilization, and which Europe can control. The West can control it if only they will stay there, if only they will remain simple tribal folks. The moment they want to get hold of, not the nineteenth-century technology to make all the mistakes the West did for another hundred years, but to leap over that and get hold of some of the modern technologies to speak their own tongue, to speak of their own condition, then they are out of place, then the Other is not where it is. The primitive has somehow escaped from control.

Well, I am not trying to help you to sleep better at night, to say it's really all right, the revolution throbs down there, it's living, it's all ok. You just have to wait for the local to erupt and disrupt the global. I am not telling any kind of story like that. I am asking that we simply do not think of globalization as a pacific and pacified process. It's not a process at the end of history. It is working on the terrain of post-modern culture as a global formation, which is an extremely contradictory space. Within that, we have, in entirely new forms which we are only just beginning to understand, the same old contradictions, the same old struggle. Not the same old contradictions but continuing contradictions of things which are trying to get hold of other things, and things which are trying to escape from their grasp. That old dialectic is not at an end. Globalization does not finish it off.

With the story about the Commonwealth Institute Photography Exhibition I tried to speak about questions of new forms of identity. But I have just barely signalled that. How can we think the notion of what these new identities might be? What would be an identity that is constructed through things which are different rather than things which are the same? This I shall address in my second talk.

39

2. Old and New Identities, Old and New Ethnicities

STUART HALL

IN MY PREVIOUS TALK, I TRIED TO OPEN OUT THE QUESTIONS about the local and the global from their somewhat closed, somewhat over-integrated, and somewhat over-systematized formulations. My argument was that we need to think about the processes which are now revealing themselves in terms of the local and the global, in those two spaces, but we also need to think of these as more contradictory formulations than we usually do. Unless we do, I was concerned that we are likely to be disabled in trying to think those ideas politically.

I was therefore attempting — certainly not to close out the questions of power and the questions of appropriation which I think are lodged at the very center of any notion of a shift between the dispositions of the local and the global in the emergence of a cultural politics on a world scale — but rather to conceptualize that within a more open-ended and contingent cultural politics.

At the end of the talk, however, I was obliged to ask if there is a politics, indeed, a counter-politics of the local. If there are new globals and new locals at work, who are the new subjects of this politics of position? What conceivable identities could they appear in? Can identity itself be re-thought and re-lived, in and through difference?

It is this question which is what I want to address here. I have called it "Old and New Identities, Old and New Ethnicities" and what I am going to do first is to return to the question of identity and try to look at some of the ways in which we are beginning to re-conceptualize that within contemporary theoretical discourses. I shall then go back from that theoretical consideration to the ground of a cultural politics. Theory is always a detour on the way to something more important.

I return to the question of identity because the question of identity has returned to us; at any rate, it has returned to us in British politics and British cultural politics today. It has not returned in the same old place; it is not the traditional conception of identity. It is not going back to the old identity politics of the 1960s social movements. But it is, nevertheless, a kind of return to some of the ground which we used to think in that way. I will make a comment at the very end about what is the nature of this theoretical-political work which seems to lose things on the one side and then recover them in a different way from another side, and then have to think them out all over again just as soon as they get rid of them. What is this never-ending theoretical work which is constantly losing and regaining concepts? I talk about identity here as a point at which, on the one hand, a whole set of new theoretical discourses intersect and where, on the other, a whole new set of cultural practices emerge. I want to begin by trying, very briefly, to map some of those points of inter-section theoretically, and then to look at some of their political consequences.

The old logics of identity are ones with which we are extremely familiar, either philosophically, or psychologically. Philosophically, the old logic of identity which many people have critiqued in the form of the old Cartesian subject was often thought in terms of the origin of being itself, the ground of action. Identity is the ground of action. And we have in more recent times a psychological discourse of the self which is very similar: a notion of the continuous, self-sufficient, developmental, unfolding, inner dialectic of selfhood. We are never quite there, but always on our way to it, and when we get there, we will at last know exactly who it is we are.

Now this logic of identity is very important in a whole range of political, theoretical and conceptual discourses. I am interested in it also as a kind of existential reality because I think the logic of the language of identity is extremely important to our own self-conceptions. It contains the notion of the true self, some real self inside there, hiding inside the husks of all the false selves that we present

42

to the rest of the world. It is a kind of guarantee of authenticity. Not until we get really inside and hear what the true self has to say do we know what we are "really saying."

There is something guaranteed about that logic or discourse of identity. It gives us a sense of depth, out there, and in here. It is spatially organized. Much of our discourse of the inside and the outside, of the self and other, of the individual and society, of the subject and the object, are grounded in that particular logic of identity. And it helps us, I would say, to sleep well at night.

Increasingly, I think one of the main functions of concepts is that they give us a good night's rest. Because what they tell us is that there is a kind of stable, only very slowly-changing ground inside the hectic upsets, discontinuities and ruptures of history. Around us history is constantly breaking in unpredictable ways but we, somehow, go on being the same.

That logic of identity is, for good or ill, finished. It's at an end for a whole range of reasons. It's at an end in the first instance because of some of the great de-centerings of modern thought. One could discuss this very elaborately — I could spend the rest of the time talking about it but I just want to slot the ideas into place very quickly by using some names as reference points.

It is not possible to hold to that logic of identity after Marx because although Marx does talk about man (he doesn't talk about women making history but perhaps they were slotted in, as the nineteenth century so often slotted women in under some other masculine title), about men and women making history but under conditions which are not of their own choosing. And having lodged either the individual or collective subject always within historical practices, we as individuals or as groups cannot be, and can never have been, the sole origin or authors of those practices. That is a profound historical de-centering in terms of social practice.

If that was not strong enough, knocking us sideways as it were, Freud came knocking from underneath, like Hamlet's ghost, and said, "While you're being decentered from left to right like that, let me decenter you from below a bit, and remind you that this stable language of identity is also set from the psychic life about which you don't know very much, and can't know very much. And which you can't know very much by simply taking thought about it: the great continent of the unconscious which speaks most clearly when it's slipping rather than when it's saying what it means." This makes the self begin to seem a pretty fragile thing.

Now, buffeted on one side by Marx and upset from below by Freud, just as it opens its mouth to say, "Well, at least I speak so therefore I must *be* something," Saussure and linguistics comes along and says "That's not true either, you know. Language was there before you. You can only say something by positioning yourself in the discourse. The tale tells the teller, the myth tells the myth-maker, etc. The enunciation is always from some subject who is positioned by and in discourse." That upsets that. Philosophically, one comes to the end of any kind of notion of a perfect transparent continuity between our language and something out there which can be called the real, or the truth, without any quotation marks.

These various upsets, these disturbances in the continuity of the notion of the subject, and the stability of identity, are indeed, what modernity is like. It is not, incidentally, modernity itself. That has an older, and longer history. But this is the beginning of modernity as trouble. Not modernity as enlightenment and progress, but modernity as a problem.

It is also upset by other enormous historical transformations which do not have, and cannot be given, a single name, but without which the story could not be told. In addition to the three or four that I have quoted, we could mention the relativisation of the Western narrative itself, the Western episteme, by the rise of other cultures to prominence, and fifthly, the displacement of the masculine gaze.

Now, the question of trying to come to terms with the notion of identity in the wake of those theoretical decenterings is an extremely problematic enterprise. But that is not all that has been disturbing the settled logic of identity. Because as I was saying earlier when I was talking about the relative decline, or erosion, the instability of the nation-state, of the self-sufficiency of national economies and consequently, of national identities as points of reference, there has simultaneously been a fragmentation and erosion of collective social identity.

I mean here the great collective social identities which we thought of as large-scale, all-encompassing, homogenous, as unified collective identities, which could be spoken about almost as if they were singular actors in their own right but which, indeed, placed, positioned, stabilized, and allowed us to understand and read, almost as a code, the imperatives of the individual self: the great collective social identities of class, of race, of nation, of gender, and of the West.

44

These collective social identities were formed in, and stabilized by, the huge, long-range historical processes which have produced the modern world, just as the theories and conceptualizations that I just referred to very briefly are what constituted modernity as a form of self-reflection. They were staged and stabilized by industrialization, by capitalism, by urbanization, by the formation of the world market, by the social and the sexual division of labor, by the great punctuation of civil and social life into the public and the private; by the dominance of the nation state, and by the identification between Westernization and the notion of modernity itself.

I spoke in my previous talk about the importance, to any sense of where we are placed in the world, of the national economy, the nation-state and of national cultural identities. Let me say a word here about the great class identities which have stabilized so much of our understanding of the immediate and not-so-immediate past.

Class was the main locator of social position, that which organized our understanding of the main grid and group relations between social groups. They linked us to material life through the economy itself. They provided the code through which we read one another. They provided the codes through which we understood each others' languages. They provided, of course, the notions of collective action itself, that which would unlock politics. Now as I tried to say previously, the great collective social identities rise and fall and it is almost as difficult to know whether they are more dangerous when they are falling than when they are rising.

These great collective social identities have not disappeared. Their purchase and efficacy in the real world that we all occupy is ever present. But the fact is that none of them is, any longer, in either the social, historical or epistemological place where they were in our conceptualizations of the world in the recent past. They cannot any longer be thought in the same homogenous form. We are as attentive to their inner differences, their inner contradictions, their segmentations and their fragmentations as we are to their already-completed homogeneity, their unity and so on.

They are not already-produced stabilities and totalities in the world. They do not operate like totalities. If they have a relationship to our identities, cultural and individual, they do not any longer have that suturing, structuring, or stabilizing force, so that we can know what we are simply by adding up the sum of our positions in relation to them. They do not give us the code of identity as I think they

45

did in the past.

It is a moot point by anybody who takes this argument directly on the pulses, as to whether they ever functioned in that way. Perhaps they never functioned in that way. This may be, indeed, what the narrative of the West is like: the notion that we told of the story we told ourselves, about their functioning in that way. We know that the great homogenous function of the collective social class is extremely difficult for any good historian to actually lay his or her finger on. It keeps disappearing just over the horizon, like the organic community.

You know the story about the organic community? The organic community was just always in the childhood you have left behind. Raymond Williams has a wonderful essay on these people, a range of social critics who say you can measure the present in relation to the past, and you know the past because back then it was much more organic and integrated. When was "back then"? Well, when I was a child, there was always some adult saying, "When I was a child, it was much more integrated." And so, eventually, some of these great collectivities are rather like those people who have an activity of historical nostalgia going on in their retrospective reconstructions. We always reconstructed them more essentially, more homogenously, more unified, less contradictorily than they ever were, once you actually know anything about them.

That is one argument. Whatever the past was like, they may have all marched forth, unified and dictating history forward, for many decades in the past. They sure aren't doing it now.

Now as I have said, the question of how to begin to think questions of identity, either social or individual, not in the wake of their disappearance but in the wake of their erosion, of their fading, of their not having the kind of purchase and comprehensive explanatory power they had before, that is what it seems to me has gone. They used to be thought of — and it is a wonderfully gendered definition — as "master concepts," the "master concepts" of class.

It is not tolerable any longer to have a "master concept" like that. Once it loses its "master" status its explanatory reach weakens, becomes more problematic. We can think of some things in relation to questions of class, though always recognizing its real historical complexity. Yet there are certain other things it simply will not, or cannot, decipher or explain. And this brings us face to face with the increasing social diversity and plurality, the technologies of the self which characterize the modern world in which we live.

Well, we might say, where does this leave any discourse on social identity at all? Haven't I now abolished it from about as many sides as I could think of? As has been true in theoretical work over the last twenty years, the moment a concept disappears through the left hand door, it returns through the right hand window, but not in quite the same place. There is a wonderful moment in Althusser's text where he says "I can now abolish the notion of ideas." And he actually writes the word "ideas" and draws a line through it to convince himself we need never use the word again.

In exactly the same way, the old discourse of the subject was abolished, put in a deep container, concrete poured over it, with a half-life of a million years. We will never look at it again, when, bloody hell, in about five minutes, we are talking about subjectivity, and the subject in discourse, and it has come roaring back in. So it is not, I think, surprising that, having lost one sense of identity, we find we need it. Where are we to find it?

One of the places that we have to go to is certainly in the contemporary languages which have rediscovered but repositioned the notion of the subject, of subjectivity. That is, principally, and pre-eminently, the languages of feminism and of psychoanalysis.

I do not want to go through that argument but I want to say something about how one might begin to think questions of identity from this new set of theoretical spaces. And I have to do this programmatically. I have to state what I think, from this position, identity is and is not as a sort of protocol, although each one could take me a very long time.

It makes us aware that identities are never completed, never finished; that they are always as subjectivity itself is, in process. That itself is a pretty difficult task. Though we have always known it a little bit, we have always thought about ourselves as getting more like ourselves everyday. But that is a sort of Hegelian notion, of going forward to meet that which we always were. I want to open that process up considerably. Identity is always in the process of formation.

Secondly, identity means, or connotes, the process of identification, of saying that this here is the same as that, or we are the same together, in this respect. But something we have learnt from the whole discussion of identification, in feminism and psychoanalysis, is the degree to which that structure of identification is always constructed through ambivalence. Always constructed through splitting.

47

Splitting between that which one is, and that which is the other. The attempt to expel the other to the other side of the universe is always compounded by the relationships of love and desire. This is a different language from the language of, as it were, the Others who are completely different from oneself.

This is the Other that belongs inside one. This is the Other that one can only know from the place from which one stands. This is the self as it is inscribed in the gaze of the Other. And this notion which breaks down the boundaries, between outside and inside, between those who belong and those who do not, between those whose histories have been written and those whose histories they have depended on but whose histories cannot be spoken. That the unspoken silence in between that which can be spoken is the only way to reach for the whole history. There is no other history except to take the absences and the silences along with what can be spoken. Everything that can be spoken is on the ground of the enormous voices that have not, or cannot yet be heard.

This doubleness of discourse, this necessity of the Other to the self, this inscription of identity in the look of the other finds its articulation profoundly in the ranges of a given text. And I want to cite one which I am sure you know but won't remember necessarily, though it is a wonderful, majestic moment in Fanon's *Black Skin, White Masks*, when he describes himself as a young Antillean, face to face with the white Parisian child and her mother. And the child pulls the hand of the mother and says, "Look, Mama, a black man." And he said, "For the first time, I knew who I was. For the first time, I felt as if I had been simultaneously exploded in the gaze, in the violent gaze of the other, and at the same time, recomposed as another."

The notion that identity in that sense could be told as two histories, one over here, one over there, never having spoken to one another, never having anything to do with one another, when translated from the psychoanalytic to the historical terrain, is simply not tenable any longer in an increasingly globalized world. It is just not tenable any longer.

People like me who came to England in the 1950s have been there for centuries; symbolically, we have been there for centuries. I was coming home. I am the sugar at the bottom of the English cup of tea. I am the sweet tooth, the sugar plantations that rotted generations of English children's teeth. There are thousands of others beside me that are, you know, the cup of tea itself. Because they don't grow it in

Lancashire, you know. Not a single tea plantation exists within the United Kingdom. This is the symbolization of English identity — I mean, what does anybody in the world know about an English person except that they can't get through the day without a cup of tea?

Where does it come from? Ceylon — Sri Lanka, India. That is the outside history that is inside the history of the English. There is no English history without that other history. The notion that identity has to do with people that look the same, feel the same, call themselves the same, is nonsense. As a process, as a narrative, as a discourse, it is always told from the position of the Other.

What is more is that identity is always in part a narrative, always in part a kind of representation. It is always within representation. Identity is not something which is formed outside and then we tell stories about it. It is that which is narrated in one's own self. I will say something about that in terms of my own narration of identity in a moment — you know, that wonderful moment where Richard II says, "Come let us sit down and tell stories about the death of kings." Well, I am going to tell you a story and ask you to tell one about yourself.

We have the notion of identity as contradictory, as composed of more than one discourse, as composed always across the silences of the other, as written in and through ambivalence and desire. These are extremely important ways of trying to think an identity which is not a sealed or closed totality.

Now we have within theory some interesting ways of trying to think difference in this way. We have learnt quite a lot about sexual difference in feminist writers. And we have learnt a lot about questions of difference from people like Derrida. I do think that there are some important ways in which Derrida's use of the notion of the difference between "difference" and "differance," spelt with an "a," is significant. The "a," the anomolous "a" in Derrida's spelling of differance, which he uses as a kind of marker that sets up a disturbance in our settled understanding of translation of our concept of difference is very important, because that little "a," disturbing as it is, which you can hardly hear when spoken, sets the word in motion to new meanings yet without obscuring the trace of its other meanings in its past.

His sense of "differance," as one writer has put it, remains suspended between the two French verbs "to differ" and "to defer," both of which contribute to its textual force, neither of which can fully capture its meaning. Language depends on difference, as Saussure has shown: the structure of distinctive propositions which make up its economy. But where Derrida breaks new ground is in the extent to which "differ" shades into "defer."

Now this notion of a differance is not simply a set of binary, reversible oppositions; thinking sexual difference not simply in terms of the fixed opposition of male and female, but of all those anomolous sliding positions ever in process, in between which opens up the continent of sexuality to increasing points of disturbance. That is what the odyssey of difference now means in the sense in which I am trying to use it.

That is about difference, and you might ask the question, where does identity come in to this infinite postponement of meaning that is lodged in Derrida's notion of the trace of something which still retains its roots in one meaning while it is, as it were, moving to another, encapsulating another, with endless shiftings, slidings, of that signifier?

The truth is that Derrida does not help us as much as he might here in thinking about the relationship between identity and difference. And the appropriators of Derrida in America, especially in American philosophical and literary thought, help us even less. By taking Derrida's notion of differance, precisely right out of the tension between the two textual connotations, "defer" and "differ," and lodging it only in the endless play of difference, Derrida's politics is in that very moment uncoupled.

From that moment unrolls that enormous proliferation of extremely sophisticated, playful deconstruction which is a kind of endless academic game. Anybody can do it, and on and on it rolls. No signifier ever stops; no-one is ever responsible for any meaning; all traces are effaced. The moment anything is lodged, it is immediately erased. Everybody has a great time; they go to conferences and do it, as it were. The very notion of the politics which requires the holding of the tension between that which is both placed and not stitched in place, by the word which is always in motion between positions, which requires us to think both positionality and movement, both together, not one and the other, not playing with difference, or "finding nights to rest under" identity, but living in the tension of identity and difference, is uncoupled.

We have then to go on thinking beyond that mere playfulness into the really hard game which the play of difference actually means to us historically. For if signification depends upon the endless repositioning of its differential terms, meaning in any specific instance depends on the contingent and arbitrary stop, the necessary break. It is a very simple point.

Language is part of an infinite semiosis of meaning. To say anything, I have got to shut up. I have to construct a single sentence. I know that the next sentence will open the infinite semiosis of meaning again, so I will take it back. So each stop is not a natural break. It does not say, "I'm about to end a sentence and that will be the truth." It understands that it is contingent. It is a positioning. It is the cut of ideology which, across the semiosis of language, constitutes meaning. But you have to get into that game or you will never say anything at all.

You think I'm joking. I know graduate students of mine who got into this theoretical fix in the seventies, one enormous French theoretician after another, throwing them aside, until they could not commit a single word to paper at all because to say anything was to open oneself to the endless sliding of the signifier. So if they said, what I think Derrida really, in — really — ooh — start again, yes, start again.

Meaning is in that sense a wager. You take a bet. Not a bet on truth, but a bet on saying something. You have to be positioned somewhere in order to speak. Even if you are positioned in order to unposition yourself, even if you want to take it back, you have to come into language to get out of it. There is no other way. That is the paradox of meaning.

To think it only in terms of difference and not in terms of the relational position between the suturing, the arbitrary, overdetermined cut of language which says something which is instantly opened again to the play of meaning; not to think of meaning always, in supplement, that there is always something left over, always something which goes on escaping the precision; the attempt of language to code, to make precise, to fix, to halt, etc.; not to think it in that way is to lose hold of the two necessary ends of the chain to which the new notion of identity has to be conceptualized.

Now I can turn to questions of politics. In this conception of an identity which has to be thought through difference, is there a general politics of the local to bring to bear against the great, over-riding, powerful, technologically-based, massively-invested unrolling of global processes which I was trying to describe in my previous talk

51

which tend to mop up all differences, and occlude those differences? Which means, as it were, they are different — but it doesn't make any difference that they are different, they're just different.

No, there is no general politics. I have nothing in the kitbag. There is nothing I can pull out. But I have a little local politics to tell you about. It may be that all we have, in bringing the politics of the local to bear against the global, is a lot of little local politics. I do not know if that is true or not. But I would like to spend some time later talking about the cultural politics of the local, and of this new notion of identity. For it is in this new frame that identity has come back into cultural politics in Britain. The formation of the Black diasporas in the period of post-war migration in the fifties and sixties has transformed English social, economic and political life.

In the first generations, the majority of people had the same illusion that I did: that I was about to go back home. That may have been because everybody always asked me: when was I going back home? We did think that we were just going to get back on the boat; we were here for a temporary sojourn. By the seventies, it was perfectly clear that we were not there for a temporary sojourn. Some people were going to stay and then the politics of racism really emerged.

Now one of the main reactions against the politics of racism in Britain was what I would call "Identity Politics One," the first form of identity politics. It had to do with the constitution of some defensive collective identity against the practices of racist society. It had to do with the fact that people were being blocked out of and refused an identity and identification within the majority nation, having to find some other roots on which to stand. Because people have to find some ground, some place, some position on which to stand. Blocked out of any access to an English or British identity, people had to try to discover who they were. This is the moment I defined in my previous talk. It is the crucial moment of the rediscovery or the search for roots.

In the course of the search for roots, one discovered not only where one came from, one began to speak the language of that which is home in the genuine sense, that other crucial moment which is the recovery of lost histories. The histories that have never been told about ourselves that we could not learn in schools, that were not in any books, and that we had to recover.

This is an enormous act of what I want to call imaginary political re-identification, re-territorialization and re-identification, without which a counter-politics could not have been constructed. I do not know an example of any group or category of the people of the margins, of the locals, who have been able to mobilize themselves, socially, culturally, economically, politically in the last twenty or twenty-five years who have not gone through some such series of moments in order to resist their exclusion, their marginalization. That is how and where the margins begin to speak. The margins begin to contest, the locals begin to come to representation.

The identity which that whole, enormous political space produced in Britain, as it did elsewhere, was the category Black. I want to say something about this category which we all now so take for granted. I will tell you some stories about it.

I was brought up in a lower middle class family in Jamaica. I left there in the early fifties to go and study in England. Until I left, though I suppose 98 per cent of the Jamaican population is either Black or colored in one way or another, I had never ever heard anybody either call themselves, or refer to anybody else as "Black." Never. I heard a thousand other words. My grandmother could differentiate about fifteen different shades between light brown and dark brown. When I left Jamaica, there was a beauty contest in which the different shades of women were graded according to different trees, so that there was Miss Mahogany, Miss Walnut, etc.

People think of Jamaica as a simple society. In fact, it had the most complicated color stratification system in the world. Talk about practical semioticians; anybody in my family could compute and calculate anybody's social status by grading the particular quality of their hair versus the particular quality of the family they came from and which street they lived in, including physiognomy, shading, etc. You could trade off one characteristic against another. Compared with that, the normal class stratification system is absolute child's play.

But the word "Black" was never uttered. Why? No Black people around? Lots of them, thousands and thousands of them. Black is not a question of pigmentation. The Black I'm talking about is a historical category, a political category, a cultural category. In our language, at certain historical moments, we have to use the signifier. We have to create an equivalence between how people look and what their histories are. Their histories are in the past, inscribed in their skins. But it is not because of their skins that they are Black in their heads.

I heard Black for the first time in the wake of the Civil Rights

53

movement, in the wake of the de-colonization and nationalistic struggles. Black was created as a political category in a certain historical moment. It was created as a consequence of certain symbolic and ideological struggles. We said, "You have spent five, six, seven hundred years elaborating the symbolism through which Black is a negative factor. Now I don't want another term. I want that term, that negative one, that's the one I want. I want a piece of that action. I want to take it out of the way in which it has been articulated in religious discourse, in ethnographic discourse, in literary discourse, in visual discourse. I want to pluck it out of its articulation and re-articulate it in a new way."

In that very struggle is a change of consciousness, a change of self-recognition, a new process of identification, the emergence into visibility of a new subject. A subject that was always there, but emerging, historically.

You know that story, but I do not know if you know the degree to which that story is true of other parts of the Americas. It happened in Jamaica in the 1970s. In the 1970s, for the first time, Black people recognized themselves as Black. It was the most profound cultural revolution in the Caribbean, much greater than any political revolution they have ever had. That cultural revolution in Jamaica has never been matched by anything as far-reaching as the politics. The politics has never caught up with it.

You probably know the moment when the leaders of both major political parties in Jamaica tried to grab hold of Bob Marley's hand. They were trying to put their hands on Black; Marley stood for Black, and they were trying to get a piece of the action. If only he would look in their direction he would have legitimated them. It was not politics legitimating culture, it was culture legitimating politics.

Indeed, the truth is I call myself all kinds of other things. When I went to England, I wouldn't have called myself an immigrant either, which is what we were all known as. It was not until I went back home in the early 1960s that my mother who, as a good middle-class colored Jamaican woman, hated all Black people, (you know, that is the truth) said to me, "I hope they don't think you're an immigrant over there."

And I said, "Well, I just migrated. I've just emigrated." At that very moment, I thought, that's exactly what I am. I've just left home — for good.

I went back to England and I became what I'd been named. I had been hailed as an immigrant. I had discovered who I was. I started to tell myself the story of my migration.

Then Black erupted and people said, "Well, you're from the Caribbean, in the midst of this, identifying with what's going on, the Black population in England. You're Black."

At that very moment, my son, who was two and half, was learning the colors. I said to him, transmitting the message at last, "You're Black." And he said, "No. I'm brown." And I said, "Wrong referent. Mistaken concreteness, philosophical mistake. I'm not talking about your paintbox, I'm talking about your head." That is something different. The question of learning, learning to be Black. Learning to come into an identification.

What that moment allows to happen are things which were not there before. It is not that what one then does was hiding away inside as my true self. There wasn't any bit of that true self in there before that identity was learnt. Is that, then, the stable one, is that where we are? Is that where people are?

I will tell you something now about what has happened to that Black identity as a matter of cultural politics in Britain. That notion was extremely important in the anti-racist struggles of the 1970s: the notion that people of diverse societies and cultures would all come to Britain in the fifties and sixties as part of that huge wave of migration from the Caribbean, East Africa, the Asian subcontinent, Pakistan, Bangladesh, from different parts of India, and all identified themselves politically as Black.

What they said was, "We may be different actual color skins but vis-a-vis the social system, vis-a-vis the political system of racism, there is more that unites us than what divides us." People begin to ask "Are you from Jamaica, are you from Trinidad, are you from Barbados?" You can just see the process of divide and rule. "No. Just address me as I am. I know you can't tell the difference so just call me Black. Try using that. We all look the same, you know. Certainly can't tell the difference. Just call me Black. Black identity." Anti-racism in the seventies was only fought and only resisted in the community, in the localities, behind the slogan of a Black politics and the Black experience.

In that moment, the enemy was ethnicity. The enemy had to be what we called "multi-culturalism." Because multi-culturalism was precisely what I called previously "the exotic." The exotica of difference. Nobody would talk about racism but they were perfectly prepared to have "International Evenings," when we would all come and cook our native dishes, sing our own native songs and appear in our own native costume. It is true that some people, some ethnic minorities in Britain, do have indigenous, very beautiful indigenous forms of dress. I didn't. I had to rummage in the dressing-up box to find mine. I have been de-racinated for four hundred years. The last thing I am going to do is to dress up in some native Jamaican costume and appear in the spectacle of multi-culturalism.

Has the moment of the struggle organized around this constructed Black identity gone away? It certainly has not. So long as that society remains in its economic, political, cultural, and social relations in a racist way to the variety of Black and Third World peoples in its midst, and it continues to do so, that struggle remains.

Why then don't I just talk about a collective Black identity replacing the other identities? I can't do that either and I'll tell you why.

The truth is that in relation to certain things, the question of Black, in Britain, also has its silences. It had a certain way of silencing the very specific experiences of Asian people. Because though Asian people could identify, politically, in the struggle against racism, when they came to using their own culture as the resources of resistance, when they wanted to write out of their own experience and reflect on their own position, when they wanted to create, they naturally created within the histories of the languages, the cultural tradition, the positions of people who came from a variety of different historical backgrounds. And just as Black was the cutting edge of a politics vis-a-vis one kind of enemy, it could also, if not understood properly, provide a kind of silencing in relation to another. These are the costs, as well as the strengths, of trying to think of the notion of Black as an essentialism.

What is more, there were not only Asian people of color, but also Black people who did not identify with that collective identity. So that one was aware of the fact that always, as one advanced to meet the enemy, with a solid front, the differences were raging behind. Just shut the doors, and conduct a raging argument to get the troops together, to actually hit the other side.

A third way in which Black was silencing was to silence some of the other dimensions that were positioning individuals and groups in exactly the same way. To operate exclusively through an unreconstructed conception of Black was to reconstitute the authority of Black masculinity over Black women, about which, as I am sure you

56

know, there was also, for a long time, an unbreakable silence about which the most militant Black men would not speak.

To organize across the discourses of Blackness and masculinity, of race and gender, and forget the way in which, at the same moment, Blacks in the under class were being positioned in class terms, in similar work situations, exposed to the same deprivations of poor jobs and lack of promotion that certain members of the white working class suffered, was to leave out the critical dimension of positioning.

What then does one do with the powerful mobilizing identity of the Black experience and of the Black community? Blackness as a political identity in the light of the understanding of any identity is always complexly composed, always historically constructed. It is never in the same place but always positional. One always has to think about the negative consequences of the positionality. You cannot, as it were, reverse the discourses of any identity simply by turning them upside down. What is it like to live, by attempting to valorise and defeat the marginalization of the variety of Black subjects and to really begin to recover the lost histories of a variety of Black experiences, while at the same time recognizing the end of any essential Black subject?

That is the politics of living identity through difference. It is the politics of recognizing that all of us are composed of multiple social identities, not of one. That we are all complexly constructed through different categories, of different antagonisms, and these may have the effect of locating us socially in multiple positions of marginality and subordination, but which do not yet operate on us in exactly the same way. It is also to recognize that any counter-politics of the local which attempts to organize people through their diversity of identifications has to be a struggle which is conducted positionally. It is the beginning of anti-racism, anti-sexism, and anti-classicism as a war of positions, as the Gramscian notion of the war of position.

The notion of the struggles of the local as a war of positions is a very difficult kind of politics to get one's head around; none of us knows how to conduct it. None of us even knows whether it can be conducted. Some of us have had to say there is no other political game so we must find a way of playing this one.

Why is it difficult? It has no guarantees. Because identifications change and shift, they can be worked on by political and economic forces outside of us and they can be articulated in different ways.

There is absolutely no political guarantee already inscribed in an identity. There is no reason on God's earth why the film is good because a Black person made it. There is absolutely no guarantee that all the politics will be right because a woman does it.

There are no political guarantees of that kind. It is not a free-floating open space because history has lodged on it the powerful, tendential organization of a past. We bear the traces of a past, the connections of the past. We cannot conduct this kind of cultural politics without returning to the past but it is never a return of a direct and literal kind. The past is not waiting for us back there to recoup our identities against. It is always retold, rediscovered, reinvented. It has to be narrativized. We go to our own pasts through history, through memory, through desire, not as a literal fact.

It is a very important example. Some work has been done, both in feminist history, in Black history, and in working class history recently, which recover the oral testimonies of people who, for a very long time, from the viewpoint of the canon, and the authority of the historian, have not been considered to be history-makers at all. That is a very important moment. But it is not possible to use oral histories and testimonies, as if they are just literally, the truth. They have also to be read. They are also stories, positionings, narratives. You are bringing new narratives into play but you cannot mistake them for some "real," back there, by which history can be measured.

There is no guarantee of authenticity like that in history. One is ever afterwards in the narrativization of the self and of one's histories. Just as in trying to conduct cultural politics as a war of positions, one is always in the strategy of hegemony. Hegemony is not the same thing as incorporating everybody, of making everybody the same, though nine-tenths of the people who have marginally read Gramsci think that that is what he means. Gramsci uses the notion of hegemony precisely to counteract the notion of incorporation.

Hegemony is not the disappearence or destruction of difference. It is the construction of a collective will through difference. It is the articulation of differences which do not disappear. The subaltern class does not mistake itself for people who were born with silver spoons in their mouths. They know they are still second on the ladder, somewhere near the bottom. People are not cultural dopes. They are not waiting for the moment when, like an overnight conversion, false consciousness will fall from their eyes, the scales will fall away, and they will suddenly discover who they are.

58

They know something about who they are. If they engage in another project it is because it has interpolated them, hailed them, and established some point of identification with them. It has brought them into the historical project. And that notion of a politics which, as it were, increasingly is able to address people through the multiple identities which they have — understanding that those identities do not remain the same, that they are frequently contradictory, that they cross-cut one another, that they tend to locate us differently at different moments, conducting politics in the light of the contingent, in the face of the contingent — is the only political game that the locals have left at their disposal, in my view.

If they are waiting for a politics of manoeuvre, when all the locals, in every part of the world, will all stand up at the same moment and go in the same direction, and roll back the tide of the global, in one great historical activity, it is not going to happen. I do not believe it any more; I think it is a dream. In order to conduct the politics really we have to live outside of the dream, to wake up, to grow up, to come into the world of contradiction. We have to come into the world of politics. There is no other space to stand in.

Out of that notion some of the most exciting cultural work is now being done in England. Third generation young Black men and women know they come from the Caribbean, know that they are Black, know that they are British. They want to speak from all three identities. They are not prepared to give up any one of them.They will contest the Thatcherite notion of Englishness, because they say this Englishness is Black. They will contest the notion of Blackness because they want to make a differentiation between people who are Black from one kind of society and people who are Black from another. Because they need to know that difference, that difference that makes a difference in how they write their poetry, make their films, how they paint. It makes a difference. It is inscribed in their creative work. They need it as a resource. They are all those identities together. They are making astonishing cultural work, the most important work in the visual arts. Some of the most important work in film and photography and nearly all the most important work in popular music is coming from this new recognition of identity that I am speaking about.

Very little of that work is visible elsewhere but some of you have seen, though you may not have recognized, the outer edge of it. Some of you, for example, may have seen a film made by Stephen

Freers and Hanif Kureishi, called *My Beautiful Laundrette*. This was originally made as a television film for local distribution only, and shown once at the Edinburgh Festival where it received an enormous reception. If you have seen *My Beautiful Laundrette* you will know that it is the most transgressive text there is. Anybody who is Black, who tries to identify it, runs across the fact that the central characters of this narrative are two gay men. What is more, anyone who wants to separate the identities into their two clearly separate points will discover that one of these Black gay men is white and one of these Black gay men is brown. Both of them are struggling in Thatcher's Britain. One of them has an uncle who is a Pakistani landlord who is throwing Black people out of the window.

This is a text that nobody likes. Everybody hates it. You go to it looking for what are called "positive images" and there are none. There aren't any positive images like that with whom one can, in a simple way, identify. Because as well as the politics — and there is certainly a politics in that and in Kureishi's other film, but it is not a politics which invites easy identification — it has a politics which is grounded on the complexity of identifications which are at work.

I will read you something which Hanif Kureishi said about the question of responding to his critics who said, "Why don't you tell us good stories about ourselves, as well as good/bad stories? Why are your stories mixed about ourselves?" He spoke about the difficult moral position of the writer from an oppressed or persecuted community and the relation of that writing to the rest of the society. He said it is a relatively new one in England but it will arise more and more as British writers with a colonial heritage and from a colonial or marginal past start to declare themselves.

"There is sometimes," he said, "too simple a demand for positive images. Positive images sometimes require cheering fictions — the writer as Public Relations Officer. And I'm glad to say that the more I looked at *My Beautiful Laundrette*, the less positive images I could see. If there is to be a serious attempt to understand present-day Britain with its mix of races and colors, its hysteria and despair, then writing about it has to be complex. It can't apologize, or idealize. It can't sentimentalize. It can't attempt to represent any one group as having the total, exclusive, essential monopoly on virtue.

A jejune protest or parochial literature, be it black, gay or feminist, is in the long run no more politically effective than works which are merely public relations. What we need now, in this position, at this time, is imaginative writing that gives us a sense of the shifts and the difficulties within our society as a whole.

If contemporary writing which emerges from oppressed groups ignores the central concerns and major conflicts of the larger society, and if these are willing simply to accept themselves as marginal or enclave literatures, they will automatically designate themselves as permanently minor, as a sub-genre. They must not allow themselves now to be rendered invisible and marginalized in this way by stepping outside of the maelstrom of contemporary history."

(Following the lecture, questions were put from the audience.)

I have been asked to say more about why I speak about the politics of the local. I did not talk about other attempts to construct an alternative politics of the global principally because I have been trying to trace through the question of ethnicity; the question of positioning, of placing, which is what the term ethnicity connotes for me in relation to issues of the local and the global. And also, because in many respects, I don't think that those attempts to put together an alternative politics of the global are, at the moment, very successful.

But the second part of the question is the more important one. Why do I only talk about what is local when the questions I seem to be addressing are, of course, very universal, global phenomena?

I do not make that distinction between the local and the global. I think there is always an interpretation of the two. The question is, what are the locations at which struggles might develop? It seems to me that a counter-politics which is pitched precisely and predominantly at the level of confronting the global forces that are trying to remake and recapture the world at the moment, and which are conducted simply at that level, are not making very much headway.

Yet where there does seem the ability to develop counter-movements, resistances, counter-politics, are places that are localized. I do not mean that what they are about are "local" but the places where they emerge as a political scenario are localized because they are separated from one another; they are not easy to connect up or articulate into a larger struggle. So, I use the local and the global as prisms for looking at the same thing. But they have pertinent appearances, points of appearance, scenarios in the different locations.

There is, for instance, ecologically, an attempt to establish a counter-politics of the planet as a single place and that, of course, is

61

important. And if I had taken the question of ecology rather than ethnicity as the prism through which I spoke, the story would have been told very differently. I hinted at that in my first talk when I said that ecological consciousness was constituting the sense of the global, and this is not necessarily entirely in the keeping of the advanced West.

So there is more than one political game being played. This isn't the only game. But if you came at it through the question of where those who have moved into representation, into politics, as it were, through the political movements that have been very powerful and important in the post-war world, and especially in the last twenty years, it is precisely their inability to connect up into one global politics which seems to be their difficulty. But when you try to find whether they are able to resist, to mobilize, to say something different to globalism at a more local level, they seem to have more purchase on the historical present. That's the reason why I concentrated the story from that point of view. But it would be wrong to think that you either work at one or the other, that the two are not constantly interpenetrating each other.

What I tried to say in my first talk was that what we usually call the global, far from being something which, in a systematic fashion, rolls over everything, creating similarity, in fact works through particularity, negotiates particular spaces, particular ethnicities, works through mobilizing particular identities and so on. So there is always a dialectic, a continuous dialectic, between the local and the global.

I tried to identify those collective social identities in relation to certain historical processes. The other ones which have been talked about are very important structurings, such as inside/outside, normal/pathological, etc. But they seem to recur: there are ways in which the other identities are lived. You know if you are inside the class, then you belong. If you are outside, then there is something pathological, not normal or abnormal, or deviant about you.

So I think of those identities somewhat differently. I think of those as ways of categorizing who is inside and who is outside in any of the other social identities. I was trying to identify, historically, some of the major ones that I think exist. If you say who you are you could say where you came from; broadly speaking, what race you belong to, a nation state of which you are a citizen or subject; you have a class position, an established and relatively secure gender position. You knew where you fitted in the world. That is what I meant, whereas most of us now live with a sense of a much greater plurality, a sense of the unfinished character of each of those. It is not that they have disappeared but they do not stitch us in place, locate us, in the way they did in the past.

Regarding a second question, as to what shifted on us: it was politics. What shifted was our attempt to understand why the scenario of the revolutionary class subject never appeared. What happened to it?

There were a few moments when it appeared. When were those? When you go back historically and look at those moments, they were not on stage as they ought to have been either. 1917 is not the subject of the unitary, already-identified Russian working class, making the future. It was not that! The Chinese Revolution is not that either. Nor is the seventeenth century, the history of the already formed bourgeoisie taking the stage. Actually, they do not take the political stage for another 200 years.

So if it is a bourgeois revolution in a larger sense, it cannot be specified in terms of actual historical actors. So, we had a way of living with that for a very long time. It is coming. Of course, it is more complex than that but the basic grid is still ok.

But then, one asks oneself, what politics flows from thinking it never really happened like that, but one day it will? After a time, if you are really trying to be politically active, in that setting you have to say to yourself: that may be the wrong question. It may be that I am not actually doing something now because I think that something in the works, some God in the machine, some law of history which I do not understand, is going to make it all right.

It is hard to describe this moment. It is a moment like waking up. You suddenly realize you are relying on history to do what you cannot do for yourself. You make a bungle of politics but "History," with a capital "H," is going to fly out of somebody's mouth at five minutes to midnight and make it all right. Or "the Economy" is going to march on the stage and say, "you have got it all wrong, you know. You ought to be over there: you are in the proletariat. You ought to be thinking that." Sort us all out, you know. And we are waiting for that moment; waiting, waiting, waiting 200 years for it.

Maybe you are waiting for the wrong thing. Not that the insights of that story, that theory, that narrative were wrong; I am not trying to throw that over. I am trying to throw over the moment of the political guarantee that is lodged in that, because then you do not conduct politics contingently; you do not conduct it positionally. You think someone has prepared the positions for you.

This is a very practical issue. You go into the miners' strike, which the British went into in the early eighties, the only major industrial showdown with the Thatcher government, on the assumption that the industrial working class was unified behind you when it was not. And you did not conduct a politics which had the remotest chance of unifying it because you assumed it was already unified.

If you said it seven times, it would be unified. So the miners' leader said it seven times. "The might of the unified industrial working class is now in a head-to-head with Thatcher." It was not. It was the wrong politics. Not the wrong struggle, but the wrong politics, conducted in the wrong way, in the light of some hope that history was going to rescue this simpler story out of the more complex one.

If you lose enough battles that way, you just do not play that game any more. You have to play it differently. You have to try and make some politics out of people who insist on remaining different. You are waiting for them all to be the same. Before you get them inside the same political movement you will be here till doomsday.

You have to make them out of the folks in this room, not out of something else called socialism or whatever it is. We made history out of figments. Suddenly you see that it is a kind of way of sleeping at night: "I made a botch of that. I lost that one." You know, the way the left constantly told itself that all its losses were victories. You know, I just won that although I lost it. Heroically, I lost it.

Just let us win one. Leave the heroism out of it. And just win a few. The next time I will be in a little bit ahead. Not two steps behind but feeling good in myself. That is a moment I am trying to describe existentially. It did not happen like that. It happened in a complicated set of ways. But you realize at a certain moment, you go through a kind of transparent barrier that has kept you in a place, from doing and thinking seriously, what you should have been thinking about. That is what it is like.

Question: Could you then say something about winning one? Could you say something about what prospect you see for rebuilding another politics, other than the one Arthur Scargill headed in the miners' struggle. And what prospect that has for breaking down that exclusivist, solidified, ego-identified consciousness?

SH: The prospects for that are not very good because the left is still stuffed with the old notion of identity, which is why I am thinking about it. It is still waiting for the old identities to return to the stage.

It does not recognize that it is in a different political game which is required to articulate, precisely, differences that cannot be encapsulated any longer and represented in that unified body. So, we do not know whether we can shift enough of that old thinking to begin to ask the question. What would a politics like that be like?

We know a little bit about it. I do think, without being romantic about it, that the period of the GLC (Greater London Council) in London was very prefigurative, but that it cannot be repeated elsewhere. It was the bringing together of groups and movements which remained the same, and yet retained their differences. Nobody who came into the GLC said "I will forget I am an activist black group because I am now in the same room as a feminist group." What you heard there was the very opposite of what we now usually think of as the conversation of a collective political subject coming into existence.

We think of a nice, polite, consensual discussion; everybody agreeing. What you heard there was what democracy is really like: an absolutely, bloody-unending row. People hammering the table, insisting, "Do not ask me to line up behind your banner, because that just means forgetting who I am." That row, that sound of people actually negotiating their differences in the open, behind the collective program, is the sound I am waiting for.

I think it did something; it opened some possibilities. It showed that it was possible. It had exactly what politics always has, which is the test, that differences do not remain the same as a result of the articulation.

One group has to take on the agenda of the other. It has to transform itself in the course of coming into alliance, or some kind of formation with another. It has to learn something of the otherness which created the other constituency. It doesn't mistake itself that it becomes it but it has to take it on board. It has to struggle with it to establish some set of priorities.

That is the sound that one is waiting for but on the whole, that is not the sound one is hearing in the politics opposed to Thatcherism. One is hearing "Let us go back to the old constituencies. Line up behind us. The old parties will come again." I do not believe it. I think Thatcherism is more deep-seated than that; it is actually shaking the ground from underneath the possibility of a return to that old form of politics. So if you ask me what the possibilities are, then the first stage of it is in our own ranks. It is quarrelling among ourselves about which direction to go before one begins to open that out.

But I do think that there are possibilities in that. I think the reason why, in spite of the fact that the GLC was never below 60–65 percent in the popularity ratings, Thatcherism nevertheless destroyed it, was because it understood its prefigurative role. It understood that if it could persist, and make some changes to the lives of a variety of different constituencies in that city, other peoples would begin to say, "Here is a different kind of model. Here is a different way to go." What would that mean on a more national scale? What would that mean in another part of the country where the constituencies are different?

I think Thatcherism understood that and it blew the GLC out of the water. It destroyed it by legislative fiat. That tells you how important they knew it actually was. Thatcherism's popularity and hegemonic reach precisely arises from the fact that it articulates differences. The numbers of people who are 100 percent with the project on all fronts are very small indeed. What Thatcherism is fantastic at is the skill of mobilizing the different minorities and playing one minority against another. It is in the game of articulating differences. It always tries to condense them within something it calls "the Thatcherite subject" but there is no such thing. That is a political representation. It is the condensation of a variety of different identities. It plays on difference, and through difference, all the time. It tries to represent that difference as the same. But do not be mistaken about it. I do not think that is so.

Conducting the counter-hegemonic politics which I have been trying to describe does not carry any guarantees that it will win. All that I am saying is that there is a difference between the politics of positionality I have been outlining and some unitary politics which is successful, which is Thatcherism. That is not the difference. The difference is between two politics of positionality; one well-conducted and one which is conducted very half-heartedly, and which is, indeed, not being conducted at all.

Thatcherism is hegemonic because it is able to address the identities of a variety of people who have never been in the same political camp before. It does that in a very complex way by always attending, through its political, social, moral and economic program, to the cultural and ideological questions. Always mobilizing that which it represents as already there. It says "the majority of English people." "The majority of the British people."

It does not have yet a majority. It is summoning up the majority and telling you that it is already a majority. And in the majority are a variety of people, people from different classes, people from different genders, people from different occupations, people from different parts of the country. That's what the Thatcherite majority is.

Next time round it will not be exactly the same. It cannot reproduce itself. It is not the essential class subject. That is not the politics of Thatcherism. Indeed, far from it; my own view is that no-one understands Gramsci better than Mrs. Thatcher. She has never read it but she does know that politics nowadays is conducted through the articulation of different instances. She knows that politics is conducted on different fronts. You have to have a variety of programs, that you are always trying to build a collective will because no socio-economic position will simply give it to you.

Those things she knows. We read Gramsci till the cows come home and we do not know how to do it. She cannot get a little bit of it off the ground. It is called "instinctive Gramsci-ism." "Instinctive Gramsci-ism" is what is beating us, not the old collective class subject.

Question: This idea of multiple identities, which you represented in some kind of "pie-chart." You gave an example of people who are Caribbean, British and Black. Is there five or ten percent or something which can be called "Humanity?"

SH: I do not think that there is. I think that what we call 'the global' is always composed of varieties of articulated particularities. I think the global is the self-presentation of the dominant particular. It is a way in which the dominant particular localizes and naturalizes itself and associates with it a variety of other minorities.

What I think it is dangerous to do is to identify the global with that sort of lowest common denominator stake which we all have in being human. In that sense, I am not a humanist. I do not think we can mobilize people simply through their common humanity. It may be that that day will come but I do not think we are there yet. Both the sources of the powerful, and the sources of the powerless, we both, always, go towards those universal moments through locating ourselves through some particularity. So I think of the global as something having more to do with the hegemonic sweep at which a certain configuration of local particularities try to dominate the whole scene, to mobilize the technology and to incorporate, in subaltern positions, a variety of more localized identities to construct the next historical project.

I am deliberately using Gramscian terms — construct the hegemonic project, the historical project, in which is lodged a variety of differences but which are all committed either in a dominant, or a subaltern position, to a single historical project, which is the project of globalization, of the kind I think you are talking about.

That is what is "universal." I think universal is always in quotation marks. It is the universalizing aspect, the universalizing project, the universalizing hope to be universal. It is like Mrs. Thatcher's "All the British people." It is a way of trying to say everybody is now inside this particular form of globalization. And at that very moment, there I am. I remain Marxist. At that very moment, whenever the discourse declares itself to be closed is the moment when you know it is contradictory. You know, when it says, "Everything is inside my knapsack. I have just got hold of all of you. I have a bit of all of you now. You are inside the bag. Can I close it?" No.

Something is just about to open that out and present a problem. Hegemony, in that sense, is never completed. It is always trying to enclose more differences within itself. Not within itself. It doesn't want the differences to look exactly like it. But it wants the projects of its individual and smaller identities to be only possible if the larger one becomes possible. That is how Thatcherism locates smaller identities within itself. You want to have the traditional family? You cannot do it for yourself because it depends on larger political and economic things. If you want to do that, you must come inside my larger project. You must identify yourself with the larger things inside my project. That is how you become part of history. You become a little cog in the larger part of history.

Now that is a different game from saying, "I want everybody to be exactly a replica of me." It is a more complicated game. But there is a moment when it always declares itself to be universal and closed, and that is the moment of naturalization. That's the moment when it wants its boundaries to be coterminous with the truth, with the reality of history. And that is always the moment which, I think, escapes it. That's my hope. Something had better be escaping it.

3. Social Theory, Cultural Relativity and the Problem of Globality

ROLAND ROBERTSON

THE NATIONALISMS OF THE MODERN WORLD ARE NOT THE TRI-
umphant civilizations of yore. They are the ambiguous expression
of the demand both for ... assimilation into the universal ... and
simultaneously for ... adhering to the particular, the reinvention of
differences. Indeed, it is universalism through particularism, and
particularism through universalism.

Immanuel Wallerstein[1]

Modern societies are characterized less by what they have in common or by their structure with regard to well-defined universal
exigencies, than by the fact of their involvement in the issue of
universalization ... The need, even the urgency, for 'universal
reference' has never been felt so strongly as in our time ... The
process of modernization is ... the challenge hurled at groups closed

---

[1] Immanuel Wallerstein, *The Politics of the World-Economy* (Cambridge: Cambridge University Press, 1984) 166–7.

CULTURE, GLOBALIZATION AND THE WORLD-SYSTEM

in by their own contingencies and particularities to form themselves
into an open ensemble of interlocutors and partners ...

François Bourricaud[2]

Like nostalgia, diversity is not what it used to be; and the sealing
of lives into separate railway carriages to produce cultural renewal
or the spacing of them out with contrast effects to free up moral
energies are romantical dreams, not undangerous ... [M]oral issues
stemming from cultural diversity ... that used to arise ... mainly
between societies ... now increasingly arise within them.... The
day when the American city was the main model of cultural fragmentation and ethnic tumbling is quite gone.

Clifford Geertz[3]

Basic Problems

The title of the symposium in which this paper was first presented
contained three key terms: culture, globalization and world-system.
Each of these is in one way or another problematic and contestable
and it is, I think, desirable not merely to identify the main problems
involved in the uses to which they may individually be put but also
to address the issue of their constituting an analytical package. To
some extent the rationale in the latter respect is provided by the
sub-title of the symposium. "Contemporary Conditions for the Representation of Identity" suggests that we should consider the ways in
which "the representation of identity" is intimately bound-up, first,
with cultural aspects of and responses to processes which can be
identified as global in their reach and significance and, second, with
an entity which has been conceptualized as the world-system. That

---

[2] François Bourricaud, "Modernity, 'Universal Reference' and the Process of
Modernization," in *Patterns of Modernity, Volume I: The West*, ed. S. N. Eisenstadt
(New York: New York University Press, 1987):21.
[3] Clifford Geertz, "The Uses of Diversity," *Michigan Quarterly*, 25, 1
(1986):114–5.

70

stipulation does indeed constitute a relatively sharp focus—and while I will not confine myself slavishly to it I will bear it carefully in mind as a directive for a general, theoretical discussion.

I begin by formulating a general position with respect to the issue of universalism and particularism in global context, to which my opening quotations draw attention. I then move to a discussion of our social-theoretical resources for the analysis of global complexity, with special reference to the concept of culture. Much of that exercise involves an attempt to loosen the notion of culture; but not to the extent that culture becomes everything and everything becomes culture, which is a strong tendency in a lot of recent work under the headings of deconstruction, postmodernism and, more diffusely, "cultural studies."

Identity and the Particular-Universal Relationship

In addition to the ideas of culture, globalization and world-system, the concept of identity is, of course, also problematic.[4] However, I cannot get involved directly in that thorny issue here. I will instead simply take the approach that, in a world which is increasingly compressed (and indeed identified as *the* world) and in which its most formidable units — namely, nationally constituted societies — are increasingly subject to the internal, as well as external, constraints of multiculturality or, which is not quite the same thing, polyethnicity, the conditions of and for the identification of individual and

---

[4] See Burkhart Holzner and Roland Robertson, "Identity and Authority: A Problem Analysis of Processes of Identification and Authorization," in *Identity and Authority: Explorations in the Theory of Society*, ed. Roland Robertson and Burkhart Holzner (Oxford: Basil Blackwell, 1980):1–39. Also see my "Aspects of Identity and Authority in Sociological Theory," in ibid., 218–65. Among the most important recent contributions to the study of national-identity formation are: Anthony D. Smith, *Theories of Nationalism* (New York: Holmes and Meier, 1983); Ernest Gellner, *Nations and Nationalism* (Ithaca, New York: Cornell University Press, 1983); Benedict Anderson, *Imagined Communities* (London: Verso, 1983); Eric Hobsbawm and Terence Ranger, eds., *The Invention of Tradition* (Cambridge: Cambridge University Press, 1983); Carol Gluck, *Japan's Modern Myths* (Princeton: Princeton University Press, 1985); Tom Nairn, *The Enchanted Glass: Britain and its Monarchy* (London: Hutchinson Radius, 1988); Harold James, *A German Identity: 1770–1990* (New York: Routledge, 1989); Hugh Kierney, *The British Isles* (Cambridge: Cambridge University Press, 1989).

collective selves and of individual and collective others are becoming ever more complex. Moreover, what Bernard McGrane calls "the authoritative paradigm for interpreting and explaining the difference of the other" has undergone mutation, so that increasingly " 'Culture' accounts for the difference of the other."[5] McGrane is concerned with "the history of the different conceptions of difference from roughly the sixteenth to the early twentieth century" — almost entirely in the West.[6] He sees a shift from "the alienness of the non-European Other" being interpreted "on the horizon of Christianity in the sixteenth century" through an Enlightenment concern with the Other as Ignorant, a nineteenth-century use of *time* as "lodged ... between the European and the non-European Other," to the twentieth-century employment of Culture.[7] This approach is important in that it draws specific attention to the civilizational bases of identity construction and representation. On the other hand, it neglects Oriental and other civilizational interpretations *of* the West — as well, for the most part, as concrete "intercivilizational encounters."[8] It also does not explicitly address the crucial contemporary question as to the emergence of a *globally* "authoritative paradigm" or globally *contested* paradigms for "interpreting and explaining the difference of the other."[9]

The overall circumstance of identity representation in conditions of great global density and complexity poses large analytical problems, to which there have been a number of responses. Among the most immediately relevant and "extreme" of these are what I will for the

---

[5] Bernard McGrane, *Beyond Anthropology* (New York: Columbia University Press, 1989) x.

[6] Ibid., ix.

[7] Ibid., x.

[8] See Benjamin Nelson, "Civilizational Complexes and Intercivilizational Encounters," in *On the Roads to Modernity: Conscience, Science and Civilizations*, ed. Toby E. Huff (Totowa, New Jersey: Rowman and Littlefield, 1981):80–106. However, Nelson did not address the issue of *the interpenetration* of *national* identities. James in his *A German Identity* has much to say about that as far as Germany is concerned.

[9] See my "Globality, Global Culture, and Images of World Order," in *Social Change and Modernity*, ed. Hans Haferkamp and Neil Smelser (Berkeley: University of California Press, 1991). Also see Roland Robertson and Frank Lechner, "Modernization, Globalization and the Problem of Culture in World-Systems Theory," *Theory, Culture & Society*, 2, 3 (1985):103–18.

sake of convenience call *relativism*, on the one hand, and *worldism*, on the other. Relativism — which term covers a multitude of "sins," including postmodernism as an ideology of the intelligentsia and "the new pragmatism" — involves, for the most part, refusal to make any general, "universalizing" sense of the problems posed by sharp discontinuities between different forms of collective and individual life.[10] In the fashionable phrases, this perspective is anti-foundational or anti-totalistic; and one of its offshoots is the view that talking about culture — certainly in global perspective — almost inevitably involves participation in a game of free-wheeling cultural politics, in which culture is regarded as being inextricably bound-up with "power" and "resistance" (or "liberation"). Worldism is, in contrast, foundational. It is based upon the claim that it is possible and, indeed, desirable to grasp the world as a whole analytically; to such an extent that virtually everything of sociocultural or political interest which occurs around the globe — including identity presentation — can be explained, or at least interpreted in reference to, the dynamics of the entire "world-system." However, that does not preclude analyzing the formation or representation of identity in terms of cultural politics; for many of those who emphasize culture as a "privileged area" at the present time make diffuse, highly rhetorical claims as to its grounding in a world-systemic, economic realm.[11]

My own argument with respect to these matters involves the attempt to preserve *both* direct attention to particularity and difference, on the one hand, and to universality and homogeneity, on the other. It rests largely on the thesis that we are, in the late-twentieth century, witnesses to — and participants in — a massive, twofold process involving *the interpenetration of the universalization of particularism and the particularization of universalism*, a claim that I will flesh out in reference to the three quotations with which began my discussion.

Speaking specifically of recent nationalism — which is, in a number of respects, paradigmatic of contemporary particularism —

---

[10] See Zygmunt Bauman, "Is There a Postmodern Sociology?" *Theory, Culture & Society*, 5, 2/3 (1988):217–38.

[11] A major example is Fredric Jameson. See in particular his "Third-World Literature in the Era of the Multinational Corporation," *Social Text* (Fall, 1986):65–88. Also see Scott Lash and John Urry, *The End of Organized Capitalism* (Madison: University of Wisconsin Press, 1987) and David Harvey, *The Condition of Postmodernity* (Oxford: Basil Blackwell, 1989).

Wallerstein insists, in my view very correctly, on the simultaneity of particularism and universalism. However, I do not think that he goes far enough in addressing the issue of their direct interpenetration, a shortfall which can be largely attributed to Wallerstein's adamance in grounding the relationship between them in "the genius and the contradiction of capitalist civilization."[12] While I think there is much to the view that capitalism *amplifies* and is bound-up with "the ambiguous expression of the demand both for assimilation into the universal and for ... adhering to the particular," I do not agree with the implication that the problematic of the interplay between the particular and the universal is unique to capitalism. Indeed, I would claim that the differential spread of capitalism can partly be explained *in terms of its accommodation to* the historical "working out" of that problematic. Nor do I agree with the argument that we can, in an explanatory sense, trace the contemporary connection between the two dispositions directly to late-twentieth century capitalism (in whatever way that may be defined). Rather, I would argue that the consumerist global capitalism of our time is wrapped into the increasingly thematized particular-universal relationship in terms of the connection between globewide, universalistic supply and local, particularistic demand. The contemporary *market* thus involves the increasing *interpenetration* of culture and economy: which is not the same as arguing, as Fredric Jameson tends to do, that the production of culture is *directed by* the "logic" of "late" capitalism.[13] More spe-

---

[12] Wallerstein, 167. Wallerstein also argues in the same passage that "capitalist civilization ... as it hurtles towards its undoing ... becomes in the interim stronger and stronger." This is undoubtedly both a more sophisticated and a "safer" point of view than that of another prominent advocate of world-systems analysis, namely, Christopher Chase-Dunn, who had the misfortune to have the following statement published in late 1989: "The revolutions in the Soviet Union and the People's Republic of China have increased our collective knowledge about how to build socialism despite their only partial successes and their obvious failures. Their existence widens the space available for other experiments with socialism" (*Global Formation: Structures of the World-Economy*, Oxford: Basil Blackwell, 1989) 342. The difference between Wallerstein and Chase-Dunn is important in that it illustrates the contrast between sophisticated and simplistic forms of "world-systems analysis." Whereas the apparent collapse of communistic socialism in 1989 must surely come as a great disappointment to *utopian* members of that school of thought, there is nothing about 1989 which should embarrass "true Wallersteinians." In fact there is a crucial sense in which it could be said that Wallerstein *predicted* the collapse of in-one-country "socialism."

[13] Fredric Jameson, "Postmodernism, or the Cultural Logic of Late Capital-

cifically, the contemporary capitalist creation of consumers frequently involves the tailoring of products to increasingly specialized regional, societal, ethnic, class and gender markets — so-called "micro-marketing."

Bourricaud, although less specific in the sense of not indicating a "driving mechanism," comes closer to the mark in suggesting that there has emerged a globewide circumstance — involving what I call the compression of the world — which increasingly constrains multitudes of groups and individuals to face each other in what he calls an "open ensemble of interlocutors and partners." This is what gives rise to *the issue* of "universalization" — and also accentuates *the issue* of particularization. Bourricaud draws attention to a critical issue which must surely lie at the center of any discussion of globalization and culture — namely, the ideational and pragmatic aspects of inter-action and communication between collective and individual actors on the global scene. This is an aspect of global "reality construction" which has been grossly neglected. However, Bourricaud does not go far enough. Missing from his formulation is concern with *the terms* in which interaction between different particularisms may occur. To him the issue of universalization is apparently a more-or-less purely *contingent* matter arising from the problem of "how to get along" in a compressed world and thus has little or no cultural autonomy — although, in all fairness, it should be said that Bourricaud is mainly trying to move us away from the purely logical or ideal solutions to the problem of world order which some of the more philosoph-ically-minded anthropologists and sociologists have offered in recent years in the face of sharp cultural discontinuities, in particular Louis Dumont.[14]

I am emphasizing two main points with respect to the interesting ways in which Wallerstein and Bourricaud have raised the universal-ism-particularism issue. First, I am arguing that the latter is a basic feature of the human condition, which was given substantial and extremely consequential historical thematization with the rise of the

---

ism," *New Left Review*, 146 (1984):53–92. For a neoMarxist, or "Postmarxist," view which gives more autonomy to culture, see Lash and Urry.

[14] Louis Dumont, *Essais Sur L'Individualisme* (Paris: Editions du Seuil, 1983). This, however, is not intended as a pejorative comment on Dumont's pioneering work on what he calls, in a very abstract sense, the major civilizational *ideologies*.

great religiocultural traditions during what Karl Jaspers called the Axial Period.[15] Those traditions were, in large part, developed precisely around what has come to be called the universalism-particularism theme and their significance in that regard has continued into our time. A major example of great contemporary relevance has to do with the way in which Japan acquired the substantive theme of universality through its encounters with and modifications, along nativistic lines, of Confucianism and Mahayana Buddhism. Japan's crystallization of a form of "universalistic particularism" since its first encounter with China has, in fact, resulted in its acquiring paradigmatic, global significance with respect to the handling of the universalism-particularism issue. Specifically, its paradigmatic status is inherent in its very long and successful history of selective incorporation and syncretization of ideas from other cultures in such a way as to particularize the universal and, so to say, return the product of that process to the world as a uniquely Japanese contribution to the universal.[16]

Second, I am arguing that in more recent world history the universalism-particularism issue has come to constitute something like a global-cultural form, a major axis of the structuration of the world-as-a-whole. Thus rather than simply viewing the theme of universalism as having to do with principles which can and should be applied to all and that of particularism as referring to that which can and should be applied only "locally," I suggest that the two have become tied together as part of a globewide cultural nexus — united in terms of the universality of the experience and, increasingly, *the expectation of* particularity, on the one hand, and the experience and, increasingly, the *expectation of* universality, on the other.[17] The latter — the particularization of universalism — involves the idea of the universal being given global-human concreteness; while the former —

---

[15] Karl Jaspers, *The Origin and Goal of History* (New Haven: Yale University Press, 1953).

[16] For an important contribution to this aspect of Japanese identity see David Pollock, *The Fracture of Meaning: Japan's Synthesis of China from the Eighth through the Eighteenth Centuries* (Princeton: Princeton University Press, 1986).

[17] See Roland Robertson, "Globalization Theory and Civilization Analysis," *Comparative Civilizations Review*, 17 (Fall 1987):20–30 and "Mapping the Global Condition: Globalization as the Central Concept," *Theory, Culture & Society*, 7, 2/3 (1990):15–30.

the universalization of particularism — involves the extensive diffusion of the idea that there is virtually no limit to particularity, to uniqueness, and thus also to difference and otherness. (One aspect of the latter tendency is conveyed by Jean Baudrillard's aphorism concerning our present condition: "It is never too late to revive your origins.")[18]

I suggest that along these lines we may best consider contemporary globalization in its most general sense as a form of institutionalization of the two-fold process involving the universalization of particularism and the particularization of universalism. *Resistance* to contemporary globalization — as, for example, some consider to be involved on the more radical side of the general Islamic movement — would thus be regarded as opposition not merely to the world as one, homogenized system but also — and, I believe, more relevantly — to the conception of the world as a series of culturally equal, relativized, entities or ways of life. The first aspect could well be regarded as a form of anti-modernity, while the second could fruitfully be seen as a form of anti-postmodernity. Put another way, it is around the universalism-particularism axis of globalization that *the discontents of globality* manifest themselves in reference to new, globalized variations on the oldish themes of *Gesellschaft* and *Gemeinschaft*. The *Gemeinschaft-Gesellschaft* theme has constituted a primary focus for the critique of modernity (most directly in Germany). It is now increasingly interwoven with the discourse of globality in the sense that it has been "upgraded" so as to refer to the relationship between the particular and the communal, on the one hand, and the universal and the impersonal, on the other. This issue is closely related to what Arjun Appadurai calls "the tension between cultural homogenization and cultural heterogenization" and which he regards as "the central problem of today's global interactions."[19]

Appadurai (1990:17) argues that "the central feature of global culture today is the politics of the mutual effort of sameness and difference to cannibalize one another and thus to proclaim their successful hijacking of the twin Enlightenment ideas of the triumphantly universal and the resiliently particular."[20] This evocative interpretation

---

[18] Jean Baudrillard, *America* (London: Verso, 1988) 41.

[19] Arjun Appadurai, "Disjuncture and Difference in the Global Cultural Economy," *Public Culture*, 2 (Spring 1990):5.

[20] Ibid., 17.

is, it should be noted, connected by Appadurai to his suggestion that "the theory of global cultural interactions ... will have to move into something like a human version of the theory that some scientists are calling 'chaos' theory."[21] While this cannot be the place for an adequate discussion of this complex issue, it should be said that Appadurai's advocacy of a *chaos*-theoretic approach to global culture — which he sees more specifically in terms of a "disjunctive" series of "scapes" (ethnoscapes, technoscapes, finanscapes, mediascapes, and ideoscapes) — clearly involves denial of the idea of the global *institutionalization* of the relationship between universalized particularism and particularized universalism.

While not rejecting the fruitfulness of Appadurai's ideas about there being empirically disjunctive relationships between different cultural "scapes" at the global level, I do insist upon the general structuring significance of the particular-universal connection — its crystallization as the elemental form of "global life." Some of my differences with Appadurai may arise from his implication that the Enlightenment ideas of universalism and particularism were necessarily incongruent. My own interpretation is that they were basically complementary. As Anthony Smith has written of the late eighteenth century, "(A)t the root of the 'national ideal' is a certain vision of the world .... According to this vision mankind is 'really' and 'naturally' divided into distinct ... nations. Each nation ... has its peculiar contribution to make to the whole, the family of nations."[22] Or, to put it more incisively, *the idea* of nationalism (or particularism) develops *only* in tandem with internationalism.

Finally, as far as fleshing-out in relation to my introductory quotations is concerned, the citation from Geertz reminds us strongly of the fact that globalization is not simply a matter of societies, regions and civilizations being squeezed together in various problematic ways but also of such occurring with increasing intensity *inside* nationally constituted societies. Nowadays, to quote further from

---

[21] Ibid., 20.

[22] Anthony D. Smith, *Nationalism in the Twentieth Century* (New York: New York University Press, 1979) 2. See also Hans Kohn, "Nationalism and Internationalism," in *History and the Idea of Mankind*, ed. W. Warren Wagar (Albuquerque: University of New Mexico Press, 1971). On a more recent period see Rupert Emerson, *Self-Determination Revisited in the Era of Decolonization* (Harvard: Center for International Affairs, Harvard University, 1964).

Geertz, "foreignness does not start at the water's edge but at the skin's ... the wogs begin long before Calais."[23] Published in 1986, Geertz's suggestions have acquired a poignant relevance to current prognoses about Eastern Europe and the Soviet Union — for in those areas the problems of old ethnic identity are being played-out within the context of increasing global thematization of ethnicity-*within*-humankind.

In any case, Geertz's observations press us, *inter re*, to take seriously into account the position of *individuals* in the globalization process. (I return briefly to the issues of multiculturality and polyethnicity raised by Geertz at a later point.) There has been a marked tendency in many discussions of the world-system, world society, or whatever, to ignore individuals — more precisely, the contemporary construction of individualism — for the apparent reason that globalization of alleged necessity refers to very large scale matters, in contrast to the "small-scale" status of individuals. This bow in the direction of the textbook wisdom which distinguishes microsociological from macrosociological approaches in terms of naive conceptions of scale and complexity is, I believe, misplaced. Thus I have in my own work insisted that individuals are as much a part of the globalization process as any other basic category of social-theoretical discourse. To be more specific, I have argued that there are, analytically speaking, four elemental points of reference for any discussion of contemporary globalization — namely, national *societies, individuals, the world system of societies* (international relations) and *humankind*.[24] My general argument in making this set of distinctions is that globalization increasingly involves thematization of these four elements of the global-human condition (rather than the world-system). (In that perspective it may be seen that there are two major particularistic elements in the world as a whole — individuals and societies — and two major universalistic elements: the system of societies, on the one hand, and humankind, the species aspect, on the other.) Any given element is constrained by the other three. For example, individuals as

---

[23] Geertz, 112.

[24] This model was first introduced, along somewhat different lines, in Roland Robertson and JoAnn Chirico, "Humanity, Globalization and Worldwide Religious Resurgence: A Theoretical Exploration," *Sociological Analysis*, 46 (Fall 1985):219–42.

such are increasingly constrained by being members of societies, members of an increasingly thematized and threatened human species and greatly affected by the vicissitudes of international relations. Thus late-twentieth century globalization involves the institutionalization of both the universalization of particularism and the particularization of universalism and can be more specifically indicated as consisting in the interpenetrating processes of societalization, individualization, the consolidation of the international system of societies, and the concretization of the sense of humankind.[25]

Returning directly to the individual, my primary claim is that globalization has involved and continues to involve the *institutionalized construction* of the individual. Even more specifically, we must recognize that world-political culture has led to a globewide institutionalization of "the life course" — which has, John Meyer maintains, two dimensions: "aspects of the person that enter into rationalized social organization" and "the public celebration of . . . the 'private' or subjective individual. . . ."[26] Much of that has been and continues to be mediated by state structures, but international *non*governmental organizations have also increasingly mediated and promoted individualism in the areas of education, human rights, the rights of women, health, and so on. In sum, the globewide encouragement of individualism in association with increasing polyethnicity and multiculturality — themselves encouraged by large migrations and "diasporations" — has been crucial in the move towards the circumstance of "foreignness" described so well by Geertz. At the same time what Meyer calls the celebration of subjective identity *relative to* involvement in "rationalized social organization" has played a major part in the virtually globewide establishment of various "minority" forms of personal and collective identification — among which gender has been of particular significance.

At the conference which has formed the basis for the present volume, and thus also of this paper, an important question was raised as to the place of women in my conception of globality and

---

[25] Elsewhere I have sketched a model of distinct phases of globalization in modern world history. See Robertson, "Mapping the Global Condition."

[26] John W. Meyer, "Self and the Life Course: Institutionalization and Its Effects," in *Institutional Structure: Constituting State, Society and the Individual*, ed. George Thomas et al. (Beverly Hills, California: Sage):243–4.

globalization. While I cannot present here anything resembling an appropriate reaction to that query, two sets of short reflections are possible. First, in empirical terms, it should be said that my own experience of the female response to the discourse of globalization is that women take to it as eagerly as men, particularly with respect to the *humankind* component of my model — the latter tendency having been confirmed to me by others, including female teachers working in the field of international (or global) studies. On the other hand, it can be reasonably argued that that "fact" should not be regarded uncritically. Is not the assignment of women to the most "familial" aspect of the globalization process a macroreplication of the historically subordinate status of women inside societies and communities? My answer to that is ambiguous — for who can tell where the maximum leverage is going to be as far as the patterning of the world-as-a-whole is concerned? Certainly the entire question of global ecology and the fate of humankind as a species will be central to the politics of the global-human condition in the coming decades. It *could* be the case that concern with humankind will be "institutionalized" as "merely" a female issue; but yet it could, alternatively, come to be a powerful basis *for feminism*. The ways in which women *participate in* the discourse of globalization is obviously the most vital factor. At this stage we do not have much to inform us. There is, most certainly, an "international" women's movement. There are also signs of serious attempts to address directly the *actual* insertion of women in the globalization process, the recent book by Cynthia Enloe being an interesting example.[27] Enloe attempts to make "feminist sense of international politics" by drawing attention to the role of women in the making of the contemporary system of international relations — as wives of male diplomats, as prostitutes for male members of armed forces, as victims of sex-tourism, as instruments of global advertising, and so on. Specifically, Enloe casts the woman as a "global victim."

---

[27] Cynthia Enloe, *Bananas, Beaches & Bases: Making Feminist Sense of International Politics* (Berkeley: University of California Press, 1990).

Social Theory and Global Culture

There seems to be something of a consensus among those sociologists who have been doing work directly on the global circumstance that the main traditions of social theory are inadequate to the task of illuminating discussion of the world as a whole and the making thereof. Wallerstein has probably put the matter most sharply in arguing that "world-systems analysis" *is a protest* against the received tradition of social science as a whole.[28] I have great sympathy with the general, if not the specific, thrust of that claim and I will now outline some of my own main views in that respect, in relation to the substantive task at hand and mainly in reference to my own "official" discipline of sociology, which has played a significant role in the actual patterning of twentieth-century globalization; but which has not, to put it mildly, done much in its mainstream to focus analytically and interpretively *on* globalization as an historical phenomenon of increasingly salient contemporary significance.[29]

There can be little doubt that sociology took its classical shape during the declining years of the nineteenth century and the first quarter of the present century in primary reference to what has come to be called the problem of modernity, on the one hand, and the mode of operation of the nationally constituted society, on the other — with the society-individual problematic being central to both. In such a perspective there was little or no room for the analysis of cultural differences except in terms of analytical contrasts between civilizations and civilizational traditions; since it was widely assumed that the modern form of society was culturally homogenous or had to become so in order to achieve viability. Obviously Max Weber had no clear sociological sense of, certainly no liking for, what we have come to call a pluralistic society. In one way or another the leading classical sociologists promoted the idea — if only implicitly — that what later came to be called a central value system was an essential feature of

---

[28] Immanuel Wallerstein, "World-Systems Analysis," in *Social Theory Today,* ed. Anthony Giddens and Jonathan H. Turner (Stanford: Stanford University Press, 1987):309.

[29] Some of the following thoughts on and documentation with respect to this subject are developed in my "After Nostalgia? Wilful Nostalgia and the Phases of Globalization," in *Theories of Modernity and Postmodernity,* ed. Bryan S. Turner (London: Sage, 1990):45–61.

viable national societies and that in external terms each society should develop a sense of its own collective identity. In that respect some sociologists of that period became very influential outside Western Europe.

Social-scientific ideas — notably those of the English utilitarians and the French positivists — had, of course, been influential among dominant, "liberal" elites in newly independent Latin American societies during the nineteenth century; but such turn-of-the-century people as Durkheim, Toennies, Spencer and Max Weber had a particular impact in European and Asian countries in terms of their ideas concerning such matters as culture and national identity, as well as those relating to the issue of what form a modern national society should take. For example Spencer — whose work was very influential in late-nineteenth century Japan and China — explicitly advised the Meiji political elite to establish a firm tradition-based Japanese identity, Durkheim's ideas on the theme of civil religion were influential in the establishment of the new Turkish republic in the 1920s, while the German theme of *Gemeinschaft* v. *Gesellschaft* (or culture v. civilization) was widely manipulated in East Asia and elsewhere. (The Meiji elite decided quite early to erect a nationally organized community — to try to have both *Gemeinschaft* and *Gesellschaft*.)

Thus even though it is conventional to think of Western social science as having developed more or less solely in the West itself (with the partial exception of its Marxian component), the fact of the matter is that in a great array of different juxtapositions it found its way into the life-courses of a large number of non-Western societies well before the peaking of Western social-scientific theories of societal modernization in the late 1950s and early 1960s (in relation to the emergence of the Third World as a global presence). By the end of the first quarter of the twentieth century Western social science had become a "cultural resource" in a number of global regions — most notably in East Asia, where there was a long-standing cultural tendency to juxtapose superficially contradictory sets of ideas in syncretic form. Thus while Western social scientists — most outstandingly Max Weber — were busy *comparing* East and West as an analytical exercise (with strong political and ideological overtones), the objects of the comparison (more accurately, intellectual and political elites) were busy sifting and implementing packages of Western ideas for very concrete political, economic and cultural reasons.[30]

The irony in this is, of course, that in spite of the diffusion of their ideas to the very societies which they were contrasting with the West there was exceedingly little sense among the leading sociologists of the classical period that an increasing number of societies around the world were in varying degrees subject — often very willingly — to their ideas concerning the functioning and operation of modern, nationally constituted societies; although those ideas were invariably recast for local purposes. In other words they had little sense of the possibility of national societies being subject to *generalized, external* expectations as to how societies could establish and maintain viability — that they themselves were actually central to the formation of an increasingly global sense of how a society should be constructed. They were, in a word, insensitive to what has come to be called globalization — particularly cultural aspects thereof.

To be sure, Durkheim became increasingly conscious of what he called an "international life" to which individual societies became increasingly subject and was actually engaged in work on the more-or-less logical — rather than the contingent-sociological — question of how culturally different societies could form an ensemble of societies in moral terms. For the most part, however, the dominant idea in the foundational period of sociology was — insofar as international or global matters were attended to at all — that societies were engaged in something like a Darwinian struggle, a view which was to be found particularly in those quite numerous societies which were directly influenced by so-called Social Darwinism and, less explicitly, in the orbits in which Max Weber was particularly influential. My main point here is thus that not merely has sociology suffered greatly from its inattention to extra-societal issues but that it still remains remarkably ill-equipped to deal with inter-societal let alone global matters, although clearly considerable effort is currently being exerted in order to rectify that circumstance. As I have said, one of its major liabilities in this regard has been its general acceptance of something like a dominant ideology or common culture thesis at the level of nationally constituted societies. And it is to that specific issue which I now turn.

---

[30] For an instructive discussion of the Japanese reception of Max Weber's ideas in Japan, see Takeshi Ishida, *Japanese Political Culture* (New Brunswick, New Jersey: Transaction Books, 1983) 51–68. More generally see ibid., 69–86.

As Margaret Archer has argued, sociological discussion of cultural phenomena has been plagued by "the myth of cultural integration," according to which all societies that are considered to be viable are normatively integrated, with culture performing the major function in that regard.[31] Archer's primary concern is to distinguish between culture as an objective, ideational phenomenon — possessing considerable autonomy in terms of its own inner "logic" (but not necessarily consistency) — from agents who, in specific circumstances, seek to comprehend, invoke, manipulate and act in reference to systems of ideas. Those analysts who consider culture to be almost exclusively of significance in terms of its capacity to *constrain* action (and social structure) are classified by Archer as "downward conflationists." The basic myth of cultural integration derives mainly from the latter, most particularly from anthropological functionalists of the 1930s, and was incorporated, in Archer's view, into sociological structural-functionalism in the 1940s and 1950s.

On the other hand, we have also, according to Archer, witnessed more recently another form of the myth of cultural integration, arising from Marxist and neoMarxist schools of thought. Deeply concerned about the problem of the persistence of capitalism, a considerable number of Marxian social scientists have produced their own versions of "the myth."[32] Archer classifies this as "upward conflationism," on the grounds that in contrast to downward conflation it involves the notion of culture deriving from and being imposed by one set of agents upon other members of a collectivity and pays little attention to the idea of culture having some kind of inner logic. In both downward and upward conflation the upshot is, to all intents and purposes, the same, in spite of differing conceptions of how the result is achieved. Culture is to be considered primarily as a constraint.

Archer also deals with a third approach, which involves the refusal or analytical inability to distinguish between culture and action (or between culture and social structure). "Central conflationism" — of

---

[31] Margaret Archer, *Culture and Agency: The Place of Culture in Social Theory* (Cambridge: Cambridge University Press, 1988).

[32] For discussion see Nicholas Abercrombie, Stephen Hill and Bryan S. Turner, *The Dominant Ideology Thesis* (London: Allen and Unwin, 1980). Also see *Dominant Ideologies*, ed. Abercrombie, Hill and Turner (London: Unwin Hyman, 1990).

which Anthony Giddens' structuration theory is provided as a major example — is actually the target of much of Archer's harshest criticism, since it leaves room neither for action in relative independence of culture nor for the objective, ideational status of the latter. In any case, my primary reason for rehearsing the central thrust of Archer's argument is that she helps clear the way for a definite sociological move away from the old culture-as-integrating approach. In particular, she draws attention to the issue of the different ways in which ideational patterns may be interpreted, employed, reconstituted and expanded under a variety of situational circumstances. On the other hand, there are, most certainly, weaknesses in Archer's *Culture and Agency*. Probably the most significant is her rationalistic bias, which precludes her from attending to expressive meaning and to morality. She also sets-up an implausible distinction between social and cultural action and does not attend directly to interaction between and interpenetration of societal cultures.

It would seem that the myth of cultural integration was, indeed, closely bound to the perception of the national society as a homogenized entity and thus it needs to be periodized just as much as does the idea of the culturally homogenous, state-governed society. In the latter respect I can do no better than invoke William McNeill, who has provided three reasons for "the prevalence of polyethnicity in civilized societies before 1750 . . . (C)onquest, disease, and trade all worked in that direction, most pronouncedly in the Middle East, and somewhat less forcefully towards the extremities of the Eurasian ecumene." In the latter "ethnic diversity diminished, though even in remote offshore islands, like medieval Japan and Britain, aliens played significant roles as bearers of special skills."[33] McNeill argues generally that the idea of an ethnically homogenous society is fundamentally "barbaric." In any case, with the French Revolution and the new conception of citizens constituting a single nation and possessing rights and duties to participate in public life, triumphed nationalism as, to quote McNeill again, "*the* central reality of modern times."[34] The major issue in the present context is whether and in what ways we can develop modes of understanding of the modern

---

[33] William H. McNeill, *Polyethnicity and National Unity in World History* (Toronto: University of Toronto Press, 1985) 33.
[34] Ibid., 34.

circumstances of polyethnicity and multiculturality, on the one hand, and globality, on the other which will not involve repetition of mainstream sociology's enchantment with the national society.

Let me emphasize in this connection that I am *not* arguing that the nationally constituted society is about to whither away. To the contrary it is being revamped in various parts of the world as the multicultural society, while "old European" and other nationalisms have reappeared — but in new global circumstances — in the context of the world-political ferment of 1989. I have, in any case, insisted that "societalism" — the commitment to the idea of the national society — is a crucial ingredient of the contemporary form of globalization (the rendering of the world as a single place).[35] Rather my point is that we should not carry into the study of globalization the kind of view of culture which we inherit from the conventional analysis of the national society. Much of our difficulty in thinking about culture at the global level stems from our experience in the latter respect — specifically conceiving of societies as unitary and larger units, including the world-as-a-whole, as lacking in such.[36] To a significant extent the unitary view of the nationally-constituted society is *an aspect of global culture.*

Apart from limitations stemming from the derivation of the notion of culture from a particularly unitary notion of society (one which was also projected by anthropologists onto primal societies during the crucial take-off phase of recent globalization, 1880–1925), the other main problem about thinking of culture in global terms derives from the fact that the dominant image of what is often called global interdependence has been centered on the global *economy* — although the self-serving idea of "the global village," promoted by television commentators remains a close and also misleading contender, as does "planet earth."

---

[35] See also John W. Meyer, "The World Polity and the Authority of the Nation-State," in *Studies of the Modern World-System,* ed. Albert Bergesen (New York: Academic Press; 1980):109–37; and Frank J. Lechner, "Cultural Aspects of the Modern World-System," in *Religious Politics in Global and Comparative Perspective,* ed. William H. Swatos, Jr. (New York: Greenwood Press, 1989):11–28.

[36] For an important critique of the unitary conception of society in a sociologically-based world-historical frame of reference, see Michael Mann, *The Sources of Social Power: Volume I, A History of Power from the Beginning to A.D. 1760* (Cambridge: Cambridge University Press, 1986).

The main difficulty with the primarily-economic attitude parallels the problem arising from our having been held in thrall by the idea of the homogenous national society. Because there has, indeed, occurred a very rapid crystallization of a global economy in relatively recent times we are tempted into thinking that that is what defines or determines globalization in general. Such a view, unfortunately, overlooks a number of historical developments which — however loosely — are bound up with the notion of global culture. Moreover concentration almost exclusively on the global economy exacerbates the tendency to think that we can only conceive of global culture along the axis of Western hegemony and non-Western cultural resistance. While it would be extremely foolish to reject the relevance of that perspective it has a number of serious liabilities.

As is well known, there has recently been considerable expansion of the rhetoric of globality, globalization, internationalization, and so on. In fact there appears to have crystallized across the world a relatively autonomous mode of discourse concerning such themes. Put another way, "globe talk" — the discourse of globality — has become relatively autonomous, although its contents and the interests that sustain them vary considerably from society to society and also *within* societies. The discourse of globality is thus a vital component of contemporary global culture. It consists largely in the shifting and contested terms in which the world-as-a-whole is "defined." To put it more specifically, images of world order (and disorder) — including interpretations of and assertions concerning the past, present and future of particular societies, civilizations, ethnic groups and regions — are at the center of global culture.

Along such lines we can readily conceive of global culture as having a very long history. "The idea of humankind" is at least as old as Jaspers' Axial Age, in which the major world religions and metaphysical doctrines arose, many centuries before the rise of national communities or societies.[37] Throughout that long period civilizations, empires and other entities have been almost continuously faced with the problem of response to the wider, increasingly compressed and by now global, context.[38] The ways in which such entities (in

---

[37] See Wagar, ed.

[38] See my "Globality, Global Culture and Images of World Order." Also see Harvey, *The Condition of Postmodernity*, 350–9, for a Marxist discussion of respons-

relatively recent history, national societies, in particular) have at one and the same time attempted to learn from others and sustain a sense of identity — or, alternatively, isolate themselves from the pressures of contact — also constitute an important aspect of the creation of global culture.[39] Even more specifically the cultures of particular societies are, to different degrees, the result of their interactions with other societies in the global system. In other words, national-societal cultures have been differentially formed in interpenetration with significant others.[40] By the same token, global culture itself is partly created in terms of specific interactions between and among national societies.

The issue of "selective response" is thus particularly important in any attempt to grasp what might be meant by the term "global culture," because it indicates the contemporary phenomenon of particular national societies becoming positive or negative paradigms as far as involvement in globalization is concerned. The *global thematization* of the Soviet-based *perestroika/glasnost* motif has played a large part in this respect. It has brought into the forefront of global discourse the problem of the relationship between societal identity and participation in the globalization process. At the same time the global popularity of the *perestroika/glasnost* motif reminds us that all societies have been under the constraint to institutionalize a connection between inwardness and outwardness.

In combination with my discussion of the universalism-particularism issue I have indicated some of the more neglected aspects of the analysis of global culture. My general argument has been that commitment to the idea of the culturally cohesive national society has blinded us to the various ways in which the world as a whole has been increasingly "organized" around sets of shifting definitions of the global circumstance. In fact it would not be too much to say

---

es to "time-space compression."

[39] For an excellent study of what is called "selective receptiveness," see Erik Cohen, "Thailand, Burma and Laos—an Outline of the Comparative Social Dynamics of Three Theravada Buddhist Societies in the Modern Era," in *Patterns of Modernity, Volume II: Beyond the West*, ed. S.N. Eisenstadt (New York: New York University Press, 1987):192–216.

[40] For a case study, see my "Japan and the USA: The Interpenetration of National Identities and the Debate About Orientalism," in *Dominant Ideologies*, ed. Abercrombie, Hill and Turner, 182–98.

that the idea of global culture is just as meaningful as the idea of national-societal, or local, culture.

4. The National and the Universal: Can There Be Such a Thing as World Culture?

IMMANUEL WALLERSTEIN

THE VERY CONCEPT OF "CULTURE" POSES US WITH A GIGANTIC paradox. On the one hand, culture is *by definition* particularistic. Culture is the set of values or practices of some part smaller than some whole. This is true whether one is using culture in the anthropological sense to mean the values and/or the practices of one group as opposed to any other group at the same level of discourse (French vs. Italian culture, proletarian vs. bourgeois culture, Christian vs. Islamic culture, etc.), or whether one is using culture in the belles-lettres sense to mean the "higher" rather than the "baser" values and/or practices within any group, a meaning which generally encompasses culture as representation, culture as the production of art-forms.[1] In either usage, culture (or a culture) is what some persons feel or do, unlike others who do not feel or do the same things.

But on the other hand, there can be no justification of cultural values and/or practices other than by reference to some presumably universal or universalist criteria. Values are not good because my group holds them; practices are not good because my group does

---

[1] I have elaborated on the distinction between these two usages of "culture" in a previous paper, "Culture as the Ideological Battleground of the Modern World-System" in Mike Featherstone, ed. *Global Culture. Nationalism, Globalization and Modernity* (London, Newbury Park and Delhi: Sage, 1990):31–56.

them. To argue the contrary would be hopelessly solipsistic and force us either into an absolutely paralyzing cultural relativism (since the argument would hold equally for any other group's values and/or practices) or into an absolutely murderous xenophobia (since no other group's values and/or practices could be good and therefore could be tolerated).

I

If I have chosen as the theme "the national and the universal," that is, if I have chosen the national as my prototype of the particular, it is because, in our modern world-system, nationalism is the quintessential (albeit not the only) particularism, the one with the widest appeal, the longest staying-power, the most political clout, and the heaviest armaments in its support.

My query is, can there conceivably be such a thing as a world culture? This may seem an absurd question, given two facts. First, for thousands of years now, some people at least have put forward ideas which they have asserted to be universal values or truths. And secondly, for some 200 years now, and even more intensively for the last 50 years, many (even most) national governments as well as world institutions have asserted the validity and even the enforceability of such values or truths, as in the discussion about human rights, concerning which the United Nations proclaimed in 1948 a Universal Declaration.

If I insist that the paradox is gigantic, it is because it is not only a logical paradox but an historical paradox. The so-called nation-states, our primary cultural container (not our only cultural container by any means, but today our primary one), are of course relatively recent creations. A world consisting of these nation-states came into existence even partially only in the sixteenth century. Such a world was theorized and became a matter of widespread consciousness even later, only in the nineteenth century. It became an inescapably universal phenomenon later still, in fact only after 1945.

Side by side with the emergence of such nation-states, each with frontiers, each with its own invented traditions, the world has been moving, so it is said, towards a world consciousnesses, a consciousness of something called humanity — a universal persona beyond even that of the so-called world religions, which in practice tended to include inside their universe only those who shared the religion.

And to top off this dual track — the historical creation of the particular nations side by side with the historical creation of universal humanity — we find a very curious anomaly. Over time, the particular nation-states have come to resemble each other more and more in their cultural forms. Which state today does not have certain standard political forms: a legislature, a constitution, a bureaucracy, trade unions, a national currency, a school system? Few indeed! Even in the more particularistic arena of art forms, which country does not have its songs, its dances, its plays, its museums, its paintings, and today its skyscrapers? And are not the social structures that guarantee these art forms increasingly similar? It is almost as though the more intense the nationalist fervor in the world, the more identical seem the expressions of this nationalism. Indeed, one of the major nationalist demands is always, is it not?, the obtaining of some form that more privileged countries already have.

This is in part, no doubt, the result of cultural diffusion. The means of transport and communication at our disposition are ever better. We all know more about what are for us the far corners of our earth than did previous generations. But it should also lead us to reflect on what pressures exist such that we are asserting our cultural differences and exclusions in such clone-like fashion?

Let us deal with two opposite modes of explaining this phenomenon that have been put forward repetitively. One is the thesis of the linear tendency towards one world. Originally, it is argued, the globe contained a very large number of distinct and distinctive groups. Over time, little by little, the scope of activity has expanded, the groups have merged, and bit by bit, with the aid of science and technology, we are arriving at one world — one political world, one economic world, one cultural world. We are not yet there, but the future looms clearly before us.

The second explanation suggests a rather different course but the outcome predicted is more or less the same. The historic differences of all groups, it is argued, have always been superficial. In certain key structural ways, all groups have always been the same. There have no doubt been several different such structures, but they make up a patterned sequence. This is of course the stage theory of human development, so popular in modern social science since its onset. Since, in this mode of theorizing, all "societies" go through parallel stages, we end up with the same result as in the theory of a secular tendency towards one world. We end up with a single human society and therefore necessarily with a world culture.

But can there be a world culture, I have asked? Not should there be one — I will return to that question — but can there be one? There seems clearly to be some deep resistance to the very idea. It takes the form on the one hand of the multiple political chauvinisms which constantly seem to resurface around the globe. It takes the form as well of the multiple so-called countercultures which also seem to surge up constantly, and whose rallying-cry, whose *cri de coeur*, always seems to be the struggle against uniformity.

I do not think that either of the two classic explanations — the secular tendency towards one world, or the stage theory of human development — are very helpful models. No doubt both capture some elements of the empirical reality we think we know, but both also disregard some very visible phenomena. And both require leaps of inference (leaps of faith?) that seem quite hazardous.

I would rather start with a model of successive historical systems in which what is certain is only that there has been and will be a succession of systems, leaving quite open what both its content and its form might be.

My basic reason for an initial skepticism about the concept of a world culture stems from the sense that defining a culture is a question of defining boundaries that are essentially political — boundaries of oppression, and of defense against oppression. The boundaries must necessarily be arbitrary in the sense that the case for drawing the boundaries at one point rather than at another is seldom (perhaps never) logically tight. Who is an Arab? What is good music? or even what is music? Is Confucianism a religion? It is clear that the boundaries depend on definitions, and that these definitions are not universally shared, or even consistent over time. Furthermore, of course, at any given time, all Arabs do not speak Arabic, all Englishmen are not individualists, some Jews and some Moslems are atheists. That is to say, it is clear that however a culture is defined, not all members of the designated group hold its presumed values or share its presumed practices. Hence, in what sense does such a group share a culture? And why are the boundaries drawn where they are drawn?

Let me begin the discussion with an example from the 10th century. At that time, a change in the social relations of production was occurring in western Europe which historians call *incastellamento* (from the Italian word for castle). It involved the building of a castle by a powerful person, who sought to use this castle as a base to force the juridical and economic submission of the local peasantry — both the freeholders and the tenant-farmers — to the seignior of the castle. These seigniors successfully asserted their right to command, to constrain, and to apprehend these peasants. What is interesting in terms of this discussion is that, as part of this process of social transformation, the terminology changed.

It seems that by the 11th century these rights that the seigniors had basically usurped by force in the 10th century were being officially termed "usages" and "customs."[2] Thus we see, in this case at least, that the word "custom," a basic term in cultural discourse, was used to describe what we know to have been a power that was usurped only a relatively short time before. In effect, calling this practice a custom was a way of legitimating it, that is, of reducing the amount of current force required to enforce it. Calling it a "custom" was an effort to transform it into a "right." The effort presumably succeeded, more or less.

No doubt, not every peasant internalized fully the idea that the dues to the seignior were the latter's "right," but many did, and most children were thereupon being socialized into this culture, even as they were also learning a given language, identifying with particular religious practices, and being taught to consider certain objects beautiful. A perceptive visitor traveling from one region to another could have described how the cultures of different regions varied. This same traveler no doubt might have noticed as well boundary uncertainties, where one culture's reach blurred into that of a neighboring culture. The more foreign the visitor the larger the arena he may have considered to constitute the boundaries of a single culture. What may have seemed a "Chinese" cultural zone to Marco Polo may have been visualized as a series of smaller zones to a merchant born within Marco Polo's "Chinese" cultural zone.

What might be called the fluidity of culture has always been a social reality, and can only have become intensified with the increasing density of human settlement. Perhaps, in 100,000 B.C. when humanity may have consisted of a series of small bands living distantly from each other, each such band was relatively culturally homogeneous. But it makes no sense whatsoever today, or even for the period of so-called recorded history, to conceive of ourselves as liv-

---

[2] See Isaac Johsua, *Le face cachée du Moyen Age* (Paris: La Brèche, 1988) 21.

ing in culturally homogenous bands. Every individual is the meeting-point of a very large number of cultural traits. If one imagined a series of groups consisting of all persons who held each of the partic-ular traits found in a single individual, each such group would be composed of a different list of persons, although no doubt there would be substantial overlapping. Still, it means that each individual is in effect a unique composite of cultural characteristics. To use a metaphor of painting, the resulting collective cultural landscape is a very subtle blending of an incredibly large number of colors, even if we restrict ourselves to looking only at a relatively small unit (small spatially, small demographically).

In this sense, the history of the world has been the very opposite of a trend towards cultural homogeneization; it has rather been a trend towards cultural differentiation, or cultural elaboration, or cul-tural complexity. Yet we know that this centrifugal process has not at all tended towards a Tower of Babel, pure cultural anarchy. There seems to have been gravitational forces restraining the centrifugal tendencies and organizing them. In our modern world-system, the single, most powerful such gravitational force has been the nation-state.

In the unfolding of the capitalist world-economy, the nation-states that were coming into existence were a very special kind of state. For they defined themselves in function of other states, together with whom they formed an interstate system. The nation-state had bound-aries that were fixed not merely by internal decree but just as much by the recognition of other states, a process often formalized in treaties. Not only did the nation-state have boundaries, but there was a very strong tendency to bound the states such that all their parts were contiguous to each other, in which case the outer boundaries of the state were constituted by a single continuous line, hopefully not containing enclaves within it. This is of course a purely formal con-sideration of political geography, but it would be a mistake not to notice how forceful and how constant has been the pressure to com-ply with such a morphology.

There was some additional de facto rules in the creation of the in-terstate system. There were to be no no-man's-lands, no zones that were not part of some particular state. And all these resultant states were to be juridically equal, that is, they were each to be "sover-eign." This presumably meant that the authorities in any state had not only full but also exclusive authority within the boundaries of the state, and that noone escaped the authority of some state.

Of course, it took several hundred years to include all parts of the globe within this system, to make each part share the same formal characteristics, and to have the volatile boundaries settle down. We are not really altogether there yet. But, compared to say 1648, when the Treaty of Westphalia was signed, consolidating the then existing European state-system, the post-1945 era of the world-system (the era of the United Nations) is a model of juridical clarity and stability.

The system as it developed was not only a system structuring state-units but also one defining the relationship of each individual to the nation-states. By the nineteenth century, the concept of "citizen" was widespread. Every individual was presumed to be a participant member of one sovereign unit, but only of one. To be sure, we have wrestled ever since with the problem of "stateless persons" as well as with that of "double nationality," but the trend pattern has been clear.

Thus were created a series of clearly-bounded entities of contiguous territory with a specified list of member-individuals. There remained the issue of how one acquired citizenship. And this issue posed itself at two moments in the life cycle: at birth, and later in life. At birth, there are really only two non-arbitrary possibilities: one acquires citizenship genetically (via the parents) or geographically (via the location of the birthplace). Though which of these methods is to be used has been a matter of constant passionate political debate, the overall trend has been from reliance on genetic inheritance to reliance on geographic rights. Later in life, there are also only two possibilities: either it is possible legally to change citizenship, or it is not. We have moved from impossibility to possibility, and the latter doubly: possibility of acquiring a new citizenship; possibility of relinquishing an old one. The codification of all of this has been complex, and the process is still not completed, but the direction has been clear.

If we take these political processes as given, then it is clear that they have posed incredible "cultural" problems. Every individual belongs juridically to one unit only, and each such unit is called upon to make a series of cultural decisions, most of them legally binding. Modern states have official languages, school systems with specific curricula, armies that require specific behavior, laws about migration across boundaries, laws about family structures and property (including inheritance), etc. In all of these arenas, some decisions must be made, and one can see why states in general should prefer uniformity whenever it is politically possible. In addition to these arenas where decisions are inescapable, there is a further arena where states could theoretically remain neutral but in practice are pressed to make political decisions. Since the state has become the major mechanism of allocating social income, the states are pressed to offer financial support to both the sciences and the arts, in all their multiple forms. And since the money available is inherently limited, the state must make choices in both the sciences and the arts. Clearly, in any given state, after 100 years of making such decisions, it is very clear that a "national" culture will exist even if it didn't exist at the outset. A particular past, a heritage is institutionalized.

But there is a second reality, which is economic. Our modern world-system is a capitalist world-economy. It functions by giving priority to the ceaseless accumulation of capital, and this is optimized by the creation of a geographically very wide division of labor, today a division of labor that is worldwide. A division of labor requires flows — flows of commodities, flows of capital, flows of labor; not unlimited or unrestricted flows, but significant ones. This means that the state boundaries must be permeable, and so they are. At the very moment that one has been creating national cultures each distinct from the other, these flows have been breaking down the national distinctions. In parts, the flows have broken down distinctions by simple diffusion. We talk of this when we speak of the steady internationalization of culture, which has become striking even in realms where it seemed least likely — in everyday life: food habits, clothing styles, habitat; and in the arts.

However, all has not been smooth in this diffusion process. People cross frontiers regularly, and not merely as temporary visitors. People move in order to work, but they do this in two different ways, or at two different levels. At the top of the occupation scale, people move regularly from rich countries to poor ones, and such persons are normally sojourners, rather than emigrants. They neither "assimilate" nor wish to assimilate; nor do the receiving states wish them to assimilate. Culturally they tend to form relatively discrete enclaves in their country of sojourn. They often see themselves as bearers of world culture, which means in fact bearers of the culture of dominant groups in the world-system.

The bigger issue is the other kind of migration, of persons at the lower end of the occupational scale, going from poorer countries to richer ones. These persons are in cultural conflict with the receiving country. They often stay permanently, or try to stay. When they wish to assimilate into the national culture of the receiving country, they are often rejected. And when they reject assimilation, they are often required to assimilate. They become, usually quite officially, a "minority."

"Minorities" are not rare today; quite the opposite. Every country has one or several; and they have them more and more. So just as there is a dialectic of creating simultaneously a homogeneous world and distinctive national cultures within this world, so there is a dialectic of creating simultaneously homogeneous national cultures and distinctive ethnic groups or "minorities" within these nation-states.

There is however one critical difference in the two dialectics. In the two parallel contradictions — tendency to one world vs. tendency to distinctive nation-states, and tendency to one nation vs. tendency to distinctive ethnic groups within each state — it has been the states which have had the upper hand in both contradictions. The states have had this upper hand for one simple reason: they have controlled the most physical force. But the states have played opposite roles in the two contradictions. In one case, they have used their force to create cultural diversity, and in the other case to create cultural uniformity. This has made the states the most powerful cultural force in the modern world and the most schizophrenic. And this is true of the states, whether we are referring to relatively powerful states like the U.S.A., France, or the U.S.S.R., or to relatively weak states like Ecuador, Tunisia, or Thailand.

II

Culture has always been a weapon of the powerful. That was what I sought to illustrate with my very brief reference to medieval Europe. But culture has always cut both ways. If the powerful can legitimate their expropriations by transposing them into "customs," the weak can appeal to the legitimacy of these same "customs" to resist new and different expropriations. This is an unequal battle to be sure, but not one that has had no effect.

What is striking about the political history of the modern world-system, as it has historically developed, is the ever more frequent and ever more efficacious utilization by oppressed elements of what might generically be called cultural resistance. Of course cultural resistance is an eternal theme. There have long been relatively stable popular cultures which have asserted their values and their forms against elite cultures. And there have long been conjunctural counter-cultures in the sense of groups who have deliberately sought to withdraw from the control systems to which they were subjected. This has often been linked with production in the arts in the form of bohemias, or with production of utopias in the form of new religions. But the conjunctural countercultures have regularly been recuperated, losing their bite. And the very stability of popular cultures has been their weakness as well as their strength. They have more often led to social anesthesia than to social revolution.

What is new in cultural resistance today is the result of the sociological invention of antisystemic movements in the nineteenth century, having the key idea that opposition must be organized if it is to succeed in transforming the world. Cultural resistance today is very often organized resistance — not spontaneous resistance or eternal resistance, but planned resistance.

Planning cultural resistance is like planning political resistance: its efficacity is also its fatal flaw. When an antisystemic movement organizes to overthrow or replace existing authorities in a state, it provides itself with a very strong political weapon designed to change the world in specific ways. But, by so organizing, it simultaneously integrates itself and its militants into the very system it is opposing. It is utilizing the structures of the system to oppose the system, which however partially legitimates these structures. It is contesting the ideology of the system by appealing to antecedent, broader ideologies (that is, more "universal" values), and by so doing is accepting in part the terms of the debate as defined by the dominant forces. This is a contradiction which a movement of political resistance cannot escape, and with which it must cope as best it can.

The same thing is true of organized cultural resistance. This is not surprising since cultural resistance is part and parcel of political resistance. If we deliberately assert (or reassert) particular cultural values that have been neglected or disparaged in order to protest against the imposition of the cultural values of the strong upon the weaker, we are to be sure strengthening the weaker in their political struggles, within a given state, within the world-system as a whole. But we are then pressed to prove the validity of our asserted (or reasserted) values in terms of criteria laid down by the powerful. Accused of being "uncivilized," the proclaimers of the (re)asserted cultural values suggest that it is they who are truly "civilized." "Civilization" (or some equivalent term) thereupon becomes the universal criterion by which one judges particular cultural acts — whether these are acts of artistic performance, or acts of religious ritual, or acts of the esthetic utilization of space and time. The planners of cultural resistance, in planning the assertion of some particular culture, are in effect (re)legitimating the concept of universal values.

The systemic cooption of cultural resistance occurs in two opposite ways, which combine to deprive the cultural resistance of its raison d'être, resistance. On the one hand, the powerful of the world seek to commodify and thereby denature the practices of cultural resistance. They create high market demand for the forms of avant-garde (and/or exotic) artistic production. They create high-tech market networks for the distribution of previously artisanal or illicit production of the means of everyday life; that is, they transform a private domain into a semipublic one. They assign public space, delimited public space, to the non-standard linguistic, religious, even juridical forms.

But it is more than a matter of mere cooption, of a kind of cultural corruption. It is as much the fact that any movement of cultural resistance that succeeds, even partially, in mobilizing significant support must deal with the consequences of what Weber called the "routinization of charisma." There are, it seems to me, only two ways to deal with the routinization of charisma. One can reduce the difference of substance to a difference of form. Thereby one may guarantee the survival of the organization that originally promoted the resistance, but at the sacrifice of the quality of its "resistance." Or one can reassert the quality of its resistance by shifting from a policy of self-assertion to a policy of proselytization. This too may enable the organization to survive, but only as a protagonist of some universal. It is the shift from proclaiming an alternative art-form, an alternative religion, an alternative epistemology to proclaiming a singular truth that deserves to be imposed.

Thus the case of cultural resistance involves the same dilemmas as resistance at the level of political power in the narrow sense. The contradictions of planned resistance are inescapable, and the movements must cope with them as best they can.

Of course, one can try to take a different tack. One can move in the direction of anarchy or libertarianism as a strategy. One can argue that the only mode of cultural resistance, the only mode of cultural assertion, that is of value is that of the *franc-tireur*, of the individual against the mass (all masses, any mass). And surely this has been tried, time and again — whether in the form of so-called art for art's sake, or in the form of withdrawal into small communes, or in the form of nihilism, or in the form of schizophrenia. We should not dismiss these diverse modes of resistance out of hand.

There are enormous advantages to these modes of cultural resistance, to which one might give the label "individualist." They are easy to pursue in the sense of not requiring the effort of organizing them, or at least requiring less effort. They are relatively spontaneous and need less to take account of dominant values. They become therefore somewhat more difficult for the authorities to control, and thereupon to coopt. They do not seek *organizational* triumph, and hence are less likely to breed among those who practice such modes the temptation to justify themselves in the universalistic language of the dominant culture. Individualistic modes of resistance are for all these reasons more total as resistance than planned social modes.

This being the case, such modes however create their own difficulties in turn. Because individualistic modes involve so much less social organization, the holders of cultural power can and do treat them either with the disdain that requires no notice, or by severe repression, which is harder to combat precisely because of the relative lack of social organization.

Thus, the individualist forms of cultural resistance have exactly the opposite advantages and disadvantages of the planned forms of cultural resistance. It is not at all clear that the balance-sheet in the end is any more positive. Furthermore, can individual resistance be called *cultural* resistance? If one pursues activities with reference only to one's inner ear, in what sense is one sharing a culture with anyone else, even with other individualist resisters? And if the answer is that the inner ear is a guide to the true path, is this not an appeal to universalist values with a vengeance, since in this case, the claim to universalism lacks any control whatsoever of social dialogue?

I have never thought, and do not think, that we can successfully escape the contradictions of planned cultural resistance by turning inward. It may be quite the opposite: it is perhaps the case that we can minimize these contradictions (one can of course never escape them entirely) of planned cultural resistance only by a *fuite en avant* of being still more social in our outlook.

III

This therefore brings us to the issue of world culture. World culture, the humanism of many sages, has long been advocated on these grounds, that it alone permits one to overcome the provincialism — hence both the limitations to moral growth, and the obscurantism — of cultural particularisms.

Let us eliminate from our discussion the naive conceptualizations of world culture, those that barely disguise an attempt to impose a particular culture in the guise of a *mission civilisatrice*. Such naive conceptualizations are to be sure commonplace, but they are an easy target of our criticism. Let us take its more sophisticated version, the advocacy of what Leopold-Sédar Senghor has called, in a celebrated phrase, *le rendez-vous du donner et du recevoir*. Can there be such a rendez-vous, and what would it look like?

In a sense, the concept of the university is itself supposed to constitute this rendez-vous. After all, the words, university and universalism, have the same etymological root. And, curiously, in medieval European usage, a *universitas* was also the name given to a form of particular cultural community. Was it then that the university in the sense of the universal was being suggested as the meeting-place of the universities in the sense of particular communities? It is certainly doubtful that this is what they have been historically, but it is regularly suggested that this is what they should become today and in the future.

The post-1968 discussion in many universities of the concept of "cultural diversity" (and its implications for curricula) is one more instance of this call. We face the very bizarre situation today of a major debate within U.S. universities between, on the one side, those who advocate a universe of cultures via the promotion of Black studies or womens' studies or the extension (if not the elimination) of the so-called canons in literature, and, on the other side, those who advocate a universal culture via the promotion of courses in Western civilization. Truly the world is upside down. One arrives, it seems to be argued by both sides, at the universal via the particular (although they differ as to which particular).

Still, is this call for cultural diversity, as Sartre suggested of Negritude, a Hegelian negation of the negation? Will not only the states, but the national cultures, wither away, sometime in the future? And if they were to wither away, is that the image at last of the good

103

society? or is it some new hell of robot-like uniformity? Would this be the fulfilment of the old anti-socialist joke: (Orator:) "Comes the revolution, everyone will eat strawberries and cream"; (Worker in audience:) "But I don't like strawberries and cream"; (Orator:) "Comes the revolution, you will have to like strawberries and cream"?

I believe we have too long avoided thinking seriously about the cultural implications of a post-capitalist future, given our quite understandable preoccupation with the difficulties of a capitalist present. Suppose it is true, as I myself believe, that there can be no liberty outside an egalitarian world, and no equality outside a libertarian world, what then follows in the realm of culture — in the arts and in the sciences? Is a libertarian world one in which everyone follows his/her inner ear? Is an egalitarian world one in which we all share equally the same universal values?

And if, as I have tended to argue here, culture is a collective expression that is combative, that requires an other, in this putative libertarian-egalitarian world, does "culture" exist?

I could retreat at this point and say I don't know, which is true. I could also retreat at this point and say that, to solve the problems of the present, the answers to these hypothetical questions can wait, but I do not really believe this to be true. It is no accident, it seems to me, that there has been so much discussion these past 10–15 years about the problematic of "culture." It follows upon the decomposition of the nineteenth-century double faith in the economic and political arenas as loci of social progress and therefore of individual salvation. Some return to God, and others look to "culture" or "identity" or some other realistic illusion to help them regain their bearing.

I am skeptical we can find our way via a search for a purified world culture. But I am also skeptical that holding on to national or to ethnic or to any other form of particularistic culture can be anything more than a crutch. Crutches are not foolish. We often need them to restore our wholeness, but crutches are by definition transitional and transitory phenomena.

My own hunch is to base our utopistics on the inherent lack of long-term equilibria in any phenomena — physical, biological, or social. Hence we shall never have a stable libertarian/egalitarian world. We may however achieve a world-system that is structured so as to tend in the direction of being libertarian and egalitarian. I am not at all sure what such a structure would look like. But whatever it might be, I assume that there would also be within its operation a constant tendency to move away from both libertarianism and equality.

In this vision of the best future I can envisage, there would indeed be a place, and a permanent place, for cultural resistance. The way to combat the falling away from liberty and equality would be to create and recreate particularistic cultural entities — arts, sciences, identities; always new, often claiming to be old — that would be social (not individual), that would be particularisms whose object (avowed or not) would be the restoration of the universal reality of liberty and equality.

Of course, this may not be a description only of a hypothetical future; this may in part be a description of the present we are living.

5. Scenarios for Peripheral Cultures

ULF HANNERZ

THE TWENTIETH CENTURY HAS BEEN A UNIQUE PERIOD IN WORLD cultural history.[1] Humankind has finally bid farewell to that world which could with some credibility be seen as a cultural mosaic, of separate pieces with hard, well-defined edges. Because of the great increase in the traffic in culture, the large-scale transfer of meaning systems and symbolic forms, the world is increasingly becoming one not only in political and economic terms, as in the climactic period of colonialism, but in terms of its cultural construction as well; a global ecumene of persistent cultural interaction and exchange. This, however, is no egalitarian global village. What we see now is quite firmly structured as an asymmetry of center and periphery. With regard to cultural flow, the periphery, out there in a distant territory, is more the taker than the giver of meaning and meaningful form. Much as we feel called upon to make note of any examples of counterflow, it is difficult to avoid the conclusion that at least as things stand now, the relationship is lopsided.

---

[1] In this presentation I draw on perspectives developed within the research project "The World System of Culture," based in the Department of Social Anthropology, University of Stockholm, and supported by the Swedish Research Council for the Humanities and Social Sciences.

We do not assume that this is the end point of these globalizing developments. The shaping of world culture is an ongoing process, toward future and still uncertain states. But perhaps one conceivable outcome has come to dominate the imagery of the cultural future, as a master scenario against which every alternative scenario has to be measured. Let us call it a scenario of global homogenization of culture. The murderous threat of cultural imperialism is here rhetorically depicted as involving the high-tech culture of the metropolis, with powerful organizational backing, facing a defenseless, small-scale folk culture. But "cultural imperialism," it also becomes clear, has more to do with market than with empire. The alleged prime mover behind the pan-human replication of uniformity is late Western capitalism, luring forever more communities into dependency on the fringes of an expanding world-wide consumer society. Homogenization results mainly from the center-to-periphery flow of commoditized culture. Consequently, the coming homogeneous world culture according to this view will by and large be a version of contemporary Western culture, and the loss of local culture would show itself most distinctively at the periphery.

This master scenario has several things going for it. A quick look at the world today affords it a certain intrinsic plausibility; it may seem like a mere continuation of present trends. It has, of course, the great advantage of simplicity. And it is dramatic. There is the sense of fatefulness, the prediction of the irreversible loss of large parts of the combined heritage of humanity. As much of the diversity of its behavioral repertoire is wiped out, Homo Sapiens becomes more like other species — in large part making its own environment, in contrast with them, but at the same time adapting to it in a single, however complex way.

There is also another scenario for global cultural process, although more subterranean; thus not so often coming out to compete openly with the global homogenization scenario. We may call it the peripheral corruption scenario, for what it portrays as a recurrent sequence is one where the center offers its high ideals and its best knowledge, given some institutional form, and where the periphery first adopts them and then soon corrupts them. The scenario shows elected heads of state becoming presidents for life, then bizarre, merciless emperors. It shows Westminster and Oxbridge models being swallowed by the bush. The center, in the end, cannot win; not at the periphery.

Biases

The peripheral corruption scenario is there for the people of the center to draw on when they are pessimistic about their own role in improving the world, and doubtful and/or cynical about the periphery. It is deeply ethnocentric, in that it posits a very uneven distribution of virtue, and in that it denies the validity and worth of any transformations at the periphery of what was originally drawn from the center. There is little question of cultural difference here, but rather of a difference between culture and non-culture, between civilization and savagery.

The global homogenization scenario may have a greater intellectual appeal than its shadowy competitor, but I think a brief exercise in the sociology of knowledge may suggest that this is because many of us share some sources of bias which contribute to making it plausible.

First of all, this scenario, too, may draw on a certain kind of ethnocentrism. The global homogenization scenario focuses on things that we, as observers and commentators from the center, are very familiar with: our fast foods, our soft drinks, our sitcoms. The idea that they are or will be everywhere, and enduringly powerful everywhere, makes our culture even more important and worth arguing about, and relieves us of the real strains of having to engage with other living, complicated, puzzling cultures. Grieving for the vanishing Other is after all in some ways easier than confronting it live and kicking.

Furthermore, the homogenization scenario is directly tied to a line of domestic cultural critique. There are surely those who see the worldwide spread of their culture as a cause for celebration, but for many of us it would be something to regret. And those at the center who have taken the greatest, reasonably consistent interest in the circumstances of life at the periphery, for some decades at least now, have usually been those who are also critically inclined toward many of the effects of the market economy back home. The homogenization scenario, then, allows the export, and globalization, of cultural critique; or alternatively formulated, bringing in fuel from the periphery for local debates at the center.

Finally, one may have some doubts about the sense of time in the homogenization scenario. If indeed there is often an idea that peripheral cultures come defenseless, unprepared to the encounter with metropolitan culture, that they are insufficiently organized and are taken by surprise, then this notion would frequently entail a measure of ignorance of the continuous historical development of center-periphery contacts. It may well be that the First World has been present in the consciousness of many Third World people a great deal longer than the Third World has been on the minds of most First World people. The notion of the sudden engagement between the cultures of center and periphery may thus in large part be an imaginative by-product of the late awakening to global realities of many of us inhabitants of the center.

Perhaps all of us began long ago to nourish doubts about the two scenarios I have identified, and would be ready on demand to improvise a critique of each. Yet some of their continued viability as constructs in the mind of the general public may depend on a lack of available alternatives, alternatives which would also offer ways of thinking and talking about what may happen at the periphery in a world of increasingly connected culture. As any such scenario that we would find reasonably satisfactory would probably have to be more complicated than these two, and thus more demanding of our and everybody else's patience, it might automatically be at some rhetorical disadvantage. Yet if it can both identify the weaknesses of the competitors and use whatever grain of truth may be in them, it might do better in long-term credibility.

As an anthropologist, I may have other biases than those which seem to be built into the global homogenization and peripheral corruption scenarios. Anthropologists are perhaps forever rooting for diversity; some would suggest we have a vested interest in it. In any case, I see the scrutiny of such scenarios, and attempts to formulate alternatives to them, as an important task for a macroanthropology of contemporary culture — not the only task, but not a very special one set aside in its own intellectual corner either. What is required is rather an overall conceptualization of contemporary culture which incorporates a sense of the pervasiveness of globalization. I also think that this is a task which one may well try and deal with in relatively general terms. Anthropologists, again, may have some predilection for variability and for the particular, exceptional, and unique, but I do not think it serves us well to respond to the scenario of global homogenization, or that of peripheral corruption, only as ethnographers with a myriad of stories. If we want an alternative to them, it had better be at a level of generality where the points of difference can be readily recognized.

Yet I would hardly be an anthropologist if there were not some concrete ethnography lurking behind my abstractions, and I should say that it is a more general familiarity with, as well as specific research experiences in, West African urban life that have done most to provoke my interest in the center-periphery relationships of world culture and to shape my gut reactions to the scenarios I have pointed to.

In a Nigerian town

Let me therefore say just something about the modest middle Nigerian town which I know best, its people and the settings in which meaning flows there. Some sixty years ago this town was just coming into existence, at a new junction of the railroad built by the British colonial government. It is a community, then, which has known no existence outside the present world system. The inhabitants are railroad workers, taxi drivers, bank clerks, doctors and nurses, petty traders, tailors, shoe shiners, teachers and school children, policemen, preachers and prostitutes, bar owners and truck pushers, praise singers and peasant women who come in for the day to sell produce in the market place. Apart from attending to work, townspeople spend their time in their rooms and yards, managing household affairs; going up and down the streets to greet one another; shopping; arguing and drinking in the beer and palmwine bars; or especially if they are young men, taking in a show at the open-air movie theater. Since about fifteen years ago, when electricity finally came to town at a time when the Nigerian oil economy was booming, they might watch TV — all of a sudden there were a great many antennae over the rusting zinc roofs. People had battery-operated record players long before, and there were several record stores, but a number of them have since closed down. The listeners now prefer cassettes, and there are hawkers selling them, mostly pirate editions, from the backs of their bicycles. People also go to their churches or mosques. (A couple of years ago, actually, a visiting preacher chose his words unwisely, and Christians and Muslims in the town proceeded to burn down a number of each other's houses of worship.)

Where meaning flows: market, state, form of life, and movement

Now let me take a round of collective human existence such as this apart, to see how culture is arranged within it. Culture goes on

111

everywhere in social life, organized as a flow of meanings, by way of meaningful forms, between people. But it does so along rather different principles in different contexts. For a comprehensive accounting of cultural flow, it is useful, I think, to distinguish some small number of typical social frameworks in which it occurs; frameworks which in part because of globalization recur in contemporary life north and south, east and west; in an African town as well as in Europe or America. The frameworks are recurrent, that is, even as their cultural contents are different. The totality of cultural process, then, can be seen within these frameworks and in their interrelations. To begin with, one may look at these frameworks in synchronic terms. But time can be made to enter in, and we can then return to the problem of scenarios, as a matter of the cumulative consequences of cultural process. All this, obviously, I can only hope to sketch roughly here.

I see primarily four of these typical frameworks of cultural process. Whatever culture flows outside these four, I would claim, amounts to rather little. The global homogenization scenario, as I have described it, is preoccupied with only one of these, that of the market, so if anything significant at all goes on in the other three, that scenario would obviously have to be marked "incomplete." But let us begin there. In the market framework, cultural commodities are moved. All commodities presumably carry some meaning, but in some cases intellectual, esthetic or emotional appeal is all there is to a commodity, or a very large part of it, and these are what we would primarily have in mind as we speak of cultural commodities. In the market framework, meanings and meaningful forms are thus produced and disseminated by specialists in exchange for material compensation, setting up asymmetrical, more or less centering relationships between producers and consumers. The market also attempts expansively to bring more and more of culture as a whole into its framework, its agents are in competition with one another, and they also keep innovating to foster new demand. There is, in other words, a built-in tendency toward instability in this framework. Let me say no more about it at this point.

The second framework of cultural process is that of the state, not as a bounded physical area but as organizational form. The state is engaged in the management of meaning in various ways. To gain legitimate authority state apparatuses nowadays tend to reach out with different degrees of credibility and success toward their subjects to foster the idea that the state is a nation, and to construct them culturally as citizens. This involves a degree of homogenization as a goal of cultural engineering. On the other hand, the state also takes an interest in shaping such differences among people as are desirable for the purpose of fitting categories of individuals into different slots in the structure of production and reproduction. Beyond such involvements in cultural process, some states more than others engage in what one may describe as cultural welfare, trying to provide their citizenry with "good culture"; that is, meanings and meaningful forms held to meet certifiable intellectual and esthetic standards. Not least would this cultural welfare provide the instruments people may use in developing constructive reflexive stances toward themselves and their world.

The state framework for cultural process again involves a significant asymmetry between state apparatus and people. It concentrates resources at the center for long-term cultural work, and the flow of meaning is mostly from the center outward.[2] In at least one current of the cultural flow which the state sets in motion the tendency may be toward a stability of meaning — the idea of the nation is usually tied to conceptions of history and tradition. But then again, we should know by now that such conceptions may in fact be spurious and quite contestable.[3]

The third framework of cultural process I will identify, for lack of a more precise term, as that of "form of life." It is surely a framework of major importance, in that it involves the everyday practicalities of production and reproduction, activities going on in work places, domestic settings, neighborhoods, and some variety of other places. What characterizes cultural process here is that from doing

---

[2] In Karl Polanyi's terminology, we may say that the cultural economy here is redistributive. See Karl Polanyi, "The Economy as Instituted Process," in *Trade and Market in the Early Empires*, eds. Karl Polanyi, Conrad A. Arensberg and Harry W. Pearson (Glencoe, Illinois: Free Press, 1957).

[3] This is in line with Immanuel Wallerstein, *The Politics of the World-Economy* (Cambridge: Cambridge University Press, 1984):162, although the main current source for this understanding is Eric J. Hobsbawm and Terence Ranger, eds., *The Invention of Tradition* (Cambridge: Cambridge University Press, 1983).

the same things over and over again, and seeing and hearing others doing the same things and saying the same things over and over again, a great deal of redundancy results. Experiences and interests coalesce into habitual perspectives and dispositions. Within this framework, too, people's mere going about things entails a free and reciprocal cultural flow. In contrast with the market and state frameworks, there are no specialists in the production and dissemination of meaning as such who are to be materially compensated for cultural work. While every form of life includes some people and excludes a great many others, there are not necessarily well-defined boundaries between them, and people may develop some conception of each other's forms of life through much the same kind of everyday looking and listening, although probably with less precision. As a whole, encompassing the variety of particular forms of life, this framework involves cultural processes which are diffuse, uncentered. The "commanding heights" of culture, as it were, are not here. As the everyday activities are practically adapted to material circumstances, there is not much reason to bring about alterations in culture here, as long as the circumstances do not change. In the form of life framework, consequently, there is a tendency toward stability in cultural process.

In contemporary complex societies, the division of labor is the dominant factor in shaping forms of life, providing material bases as well as central experiences. But as the reciprocity and redundancy of the flow of meaning between people involved with one another at work, in domesticity and in sociability seem similar enough, I think of this as a single framework.

Looking now at my Nigerian town, or at peripheral societies generally, one can see that the variety of forms of life are drawn into the world system in somewhat different ways, as the local division of labor is entangled with the international division of labor. There are still people, fairly self-sufficient agriculturalists in the vicinity of the town, who seem only rather incompletely integrated into the world system in material terms: who just barely make it into the periphery. On the other hand, there are people like the railroad employees whose mode of existence is based on the fact that the desire arose, some time early in this century, to carry tin and groundnuts from inland Nigeria to the world.

But then also some forms of life more than others become defined, with precision and overall, in terms of culture which has flown and continues to flow from center to periphery. It is true that through their livelihoods at least, the peasant women who come to market in the Nigerian town, or the praise singer who performs for local notables, are not very much involved with metropolitan meaning systems; the railroader, the bank clerk and the doctor are rather more. Yet there is no one-to-one relationship either between the specificity of such cultural definition and degree of world system material involvement. In many places on the periphery, there are forms of life owing their material existence, such as it may be, very immediately to the world system — forms of life revolving around oil wells, copper mines, coffee plantations. And yet the plantation worker may earn his living with a relative minimum of particular technological or organizational skills originating at the center.

To the extent that forms of life, or segments of the daily round which they encompass, are not subjected to any higher degree of cultural definition from the center, by way of the international division of labor or otherwise, there is room for more cultural autonomy. And of course, the strength of the culture existing in such reserves may be such that it also reaches back to penetrate into segments more directly and more extensively defined by the center. This is putting things very briefly; we come back to the implications.

For the fourth and final framework of cultural process in contemporary life I would nominate that of movements, more intermittently part of the cultural totality than the other three, although it can hardly be gainsaid that especially in the last quarter-century or so, they have had a major influence — examples of this being the women's movement, the environmental movement, and the peace movement. In the present context of considering center-periphery links of culture, I will say less about the movement framework, however, and mention it here mostly for the sake of completeness.[4] It is undoubt-

---

[4] Movements tend to be less centralized in their management of the cultural flow than what we usually find in the state and market frameworks, and there is also less concentration of material resources. In this they are more like forms of life, out of which they of course tend to emerge as people within the latter become dissatisfied with existing conditions or are threatened by changes. As compared with what goes on within the form of life framework itself, on the other hand, movements foster a more deliberate and explicit flow of meaning, and are more outward-oriented, missionizing. Insofar as they are oriented toward specific changes or toward averting such changes, they are also more inherently unstable — they tend to succeed or fail.

115

edly true, as Roland Robertson notes,[5] that globalization often forms an important part of the background for the rise of contemporary movements. Yet it seems to me that the great transnational movements of recent times have not in themselves seemed to become fully organized in a reach all the way between center and periphery. Some rather combine center and semi-periphery, others parts of the periphery.

Market, state, form of life and movement can be rather commonsensically distinguished, but we see that they differ in their centering and decentering tendencies, in their politics of culture and in their cultural economies. They also have their own tendencies with respect to the temporal dimension of culture. At the same time, it is true that much of what goes on in culture has to do with their interrelations. States, markets and movements are ultimately only successful if they can get forms of life to open up to them. States sometimes compete in markets; nationalist movements have been known to transform themselves into states; some movements create internal markets, and they can be newsworthy and thus commoditizable in the market; forms of life can be selectively commoditized as life style news; and so on, indefinitely. These entanglements, involving often mutually contradictory tendencies, keep the totality alive, shifting, continuously unstable.

The frameworks at the periphery

Apart from what I have already said about forms of life, then, what are the characteristics of the frameworks and their interrelations in the cultural process of the periphery, and how do they affect the way the periphery is drawn into world culture, now and in the future? What is not least significant here are the different although internally diverse ways in which the frameworks relate to space.

The connection between cultural process and territory, we should remind ourselves here, is only contingent. As socially organized meaning, culture is primarily a phenomenon of interaction, and only

---

[5] Roland Robertson, "Globality, Global Culture and Images of World Order," in *Social Change and Modernity*, eds. Hans Haverkamp and Neil Smelser (Berkeley: University of California Press, 1991).

if interactions are tied to particular spaces is culture likewise so. When culture, as in the works of classical anthropology, was altogether a matter of a flow of meaning in face-to-face relationships between people who do not move around much, it could be a simple enough matter to think of cultures in the plural as entities located in territories. When cultural technology allows alternatives to face-to-face contacts and when people become increasingly footloose anyway, then it all gets more complicated. With the globalization of culture, that is certainly where we are now.

But to reiterate, the frameworks for cultural process relate differently to territoriality. As the state is in itself an organization of territory, this is the framework in which there is the greatest vested interest in a spatial definition of culture. Even where the state as an agent is closely coordinated with the agents of a transnational market economy, it is likely to maintain some of its autonomy of action, some of its effectiveness and indispensability as a broker between the transnational and the local, through appeals in which the idea of the nation mediates between state and form of life. This may entail some disregard for, or even suppression of, the diversity of forms of life existing within the territorial boundaries of the state. Looking outward, it is in the peripheral state apparatuses that what within the transnational market framework is called "the free flow of information" meets with most resistance, and it is from there that "a new international information order" is proposed to constrain it. And it is likewise within the peripheral state apparatuses that campaigns for national distinctiveness often emanate — away with miniskirts, neckties and Christian names, in with presidential hippopotamus-hide flywhisks and the management of tradition by "cultural animateurs" employed by the Ministry of Culture or the district commissioner.[6]

Some peripheral states do more with this than others. Nigeria, with its rather deep internal cleavages and a rapid turnover of political regimes, has not used its state apparatus very insistently or consistently for such promotional efforts — the prime example that would come to the mind of an Africanist would rather be the Zairean "authenticity" campaigns of Mobutu Sese Seko.[7]

---

[6] On "cultural animateurs," see Roy Shaw, "The Cultural 'Animateur' in Contemporary Society," *Cahiers d'Histoire Mondiale*, 14 (1972):460–72.

[7] On authenticity in Zaire, see Thomas M. Callaghy, "State-Subject Communi-

World-system theory in the Wallersteinian version, as I have so far understood it, may not have had much time for culture at all, but when culture has entered in, mostly as a matter of ideology and a manipulative use of tradition, it is this kind of spatial ordering of it, to bound periphery from center, which has been emphasized. Yet the part of the state in the global organization of culture is certainly ambiguous and contradictory. Contemporary state forms, and contemporary ideas of nation and nationalism, are themselves in large part items of transnational diffusion. And for the peripheral state, to provide for the material welfare of its citizenry and to stay in business as a competitor within the international system, it has had to be heavily involved in the wholesale importation of culture from center to periphery. As it reconstructs society within its territory into a form which is more or less globally recurrent, institutions are introduced which are fundamentally inspired by and modeled on those of the world system centers. Moreover, these institutions require standardized competences, guaranteed by educational systems which are at least in principle, in terms of their objectives, remarkably uniform between states. The schools, indeed, are the most conspicuous means by which the state-organized flow of culture reaches into the Nigerian town.

Forms of life vary in the strength of their territorial anchorage. The daily round of activities for some people may still remain in one place, over a lifetime. But for others it is a matter of much coming and going. In contemporary Nigerian urban life, one of the recurrent events of the ritual order is the sendoff party — and while in a small town like the one I have described, the civil servants or bank clerks or teachers or students may not be likely to be transferred very far and usually stay in Nigeria, if you go to a larger city you will run into the cosmopolitan entrepreneurs, managers, professionals and intellectuals, the jet set and perhaps potential brain drain, often staying conveniently close to an international airport, but also constantly maintaining contact with the center through the written word or other media. Here the form of life makes the link between culture

---

cation in Zaire: Domination and the Concept of Domain Consensus," *Journal of Modern African Studies*, 18 (1980):469–492; for a portrayal of its re-exported form in Togo, see George Packer, *The Village of Waiting* (New York: Vintage, 1988):101ff.

and territory rather tenuous; and one may observe that the state, as it culturally constructs people to take up the positions in question within the division of labor, and insofar as it also constitutes much of that division of labor itself, ensures that there will be people whose horizons transcend its own territorial boundaries.

Within the market framework, in line with the scenario of global homogenization, we may expect the link between territory and cultural process to be rather weak. National boundaries may be ignored, subverted or devalued, rather than celebrated. Some transnational cultural commodity flow is indeed based on minimal attention to any particular, differentiated characteristics on the part of consumers. This is true of what Karin Barber, in an overview of African popular culture, has aptly called "cultural dumping" — "akin to the dumping of expired drugs and non-functional buses."[8]

The cost of taking old westerns, soap serials or skin flicks (to choose only examples from the screen) to their final burial place at the periphery is so low that whatever they may earn is almost pure profit; an unanticipated addition to what they made in those markets for which they were actually produced. The global homogenization scenario takes a special, perhaps temporary twist here: the periphery is seen to be for the time being not really different, but backward and third-rate. So it can be treated to leftovers.

If there is one tendency within the market framework to homogenize and reach as widely as possible with the same single product, however, there is also the alternative of limiting the competition by finding a particular niche for a more specialized product. In focusing on the market as the major force of global homogenization, one of our scenarios for peripheral cultures rather too much ignores this alternative. But since that scenario is so often preoccupied with the commodities of popular culture, whether in the form of music, television, film, fashion or the written word, let us observe that much of what the entrepreneurs of popular culture in the Third World are doing these days involves carving out such niches: nobody with any experience of West African urban life can fail to be impressed with the continuously changing variety of popular music — highlife, juju, Afrobeat, apala or whatever. Peter Manuel, in his ethnomusicological

---

[8] Karin Barber, "Popular Arts in Africa," *African Studies Review*, 30 (1987) 3: 1–18.

survey of the field, concludes that "it may seem that every prominent West African musician has coined some label for his particular fusion of traditional and modern sounds."[9] On Nigerian television, a large part of the programming is indeed a matter of cultural dumping, old American serials which those of us who are at the center may barely even remember any longer. But in my Nigerian town, it seemed that they often drew little attention or involvement. What engaged viewers, and this is also what the beginnings of Nigerian media research suggest, were the Nigerian sitcoms, showing incidents and people of a more familiar kind.[10] I note also what Karin Barber says about movie-going in small towns in southwestern Nigeria. Some years ago, the theaters showed mostly American, Hongkong or Indian films, but according to Barber, they have now become increasingly hard to find. Locally produced films, in the language of the area and using the personnel, style and themes of a well-established tradition of traveling popular theater, have replaced the imports.

These entrepreneurs may not have the material resources of the culture businesses of the center, but like local entrepreneurs anywhere, they know their territory; their particular asset is cultural competence, cultural sensibility. And this derives from an involvement with local forms of life. Coming out of these themselves, indeed being still in them, they are tuned in to the tastes and concerns which can provide markets for particular commodities, and thus niches for their enterprises. To a degree this may entail commoditizing meanings and cultural forms which were previously contained within the free-flow cultural economy of a form of life, but often this is only made possible through their incorporation into new syntheses with technology, organizational forms, and modes of expression drawn from the global flow of culture.

Which is to say that this flow does not necessarily constitute an indivisible whole. Along the way, somewhere, it can be unpacked as a multitude of separate parts — the cultural technology, such as media or musical instruments; the symbolic forms or genres through which

---

[9] Peter Manuel, *Popular Musics of the Non-Western World* (New York: Oxford University Press, 1988).

[10] See O. O. Oreh, "*Masquerade* and other Plays on Nigerian Television" and Theo Vincent, "Television Drama in Nigeria: A Critical Assessment," in *Mass Communication, Culture and Society in West Africa*, ed. Frank Okwu Ugboajah (Munich: Hans Zell/K. G. Saur, 1985).

meanings can be communicated; the meanings themselves. And where they are taken apart, they can also be assembled in new ways, combined with parts of other, often local derivation. At which times some of the imported components may certainly also be discarded, as rubbish.

Perhaps so much of this creativity passes quite neglected in the global homogenization scenario for the twin reasons that from a vantage point at the center, many of us really do not see it, and since it is so much a phenomenon of the market, some prefer not to see it. Yet it is there in the arenas where the force of global homogenization is usually taken to be at its strongest, and it often seems to compete with considerable success.

Prospects: saturation and maturation

Let me approach now the question of longer-term trends of cultural process at the periphery. The interactions between the several frameworks of cultural process depend on their respective contents and modes of organization as well as their relative strengths, which may change over time. The movement framework, about which I have said least here, obviously waxes and wanes. The state, especially apart from what it does in the field of education, is quite variably strong. It may speak in a very loud voice in its celebration of national ideology, or it may be barely audible. With regard to what I described before as policies of cultural welfare, one has to be especially aware that peripheral states are often what Gunnar Myrdal some twenty years ago described as "soft states," with very limited capacity for policy implementation.[11] This tends to be obvious enough in the area of cultural policy.

Clearly the performance of the state in managing cultural flow depends in some significant part on material conditions. The soft state is often an impoverished state which may ill afford to maintain a powerful cultural apparatus. The factor of material bases is no less important within the market framework — when culture is commoditized, it has to be materially compensated for.

This simple but fundamental fact seems often to be treated in a

---

[11] Gunnar Myrdal, *Asian Drama* (New York: Pantheon, 1968).

rather cavalier manner within the global homogenization scenario. One would have to take a range of possibilities into account here. If the involvement of the periphery with the international division of labor is not to its advantage, at any one time or over time, this would rather suggest that the periphery through its involvement with the world system becomes a poorer market for a transnational flow of cultural commodities; with the possible exception of what we have labeled "cultural dumping," which may involve low, affordable prices, but otherwise often unattractive goods. Conversely, of course, if some part of the periphery becomes nouveau riche, it may be flooded with the cultural commodities of the center. In recent times, again, the economies of some parts of the periphery, including Nigeria, have been on a rollercoaster ride, and it is not altogether obvious what are the longer term implications of such shifts in the cultural market. One question is certainly at what points local entrepreneurs will become more active in import substitution, and in what form.

There are noteworthy uncertainties here, then, which we have to bear in mind even as we try to think of what may be trends of cumulative change. This much granted, I propose that it may be useful to identify two tendencies in the longer-term reconstruction of peripheral cultures within the global ecumene. One might think of each (although as will be noted later, I prefer not to) as a distinctive scenario of future cultural history, and in these terms they would bear some resemblance to the global homogenization scenario and the peripheral corruption scenarios respectively.

I will call one the saturation tendency, and the other the maturation tendency. The saturation tendency is that which may be seen as a version of the global homogenization scenario, with some more detailed interest in historical sequence. It would suggest that as the transnational cultural influences, of whatever sort but in large part certainly market organized, and operating in a continuously open structure, unendingly pound on the sensibilities of the people of the periphery, peripheral culture will step by step assimilate more and more of the imported meanings and forms, becoming gradually indistinguishable from the center. At any one time, what is considered local culture is a little more penetrated by transnational forms than what went before it as local culture, although at any one time, until the end point is reached, the contrast between local and transnational may still be drawn, and still be regarded as significant. The cultural

122

differences celebrated and recommended for safeguarding now may only be a pale reflection of what once existed, and sooner or later they will be gone as well.

What is suggested here is that the center, through the frameworks of cultural process within which the transnational flow passes most readily, and among which the market framework is certainly conspicuous, cumulatively colonizes the minds of the periphery, with a corresponding institutionalization of its forms, getting the periphery so "hooked" that soon enough there is no real opportunity for choice. The mere fact that these forms originate in the center makes them even more attractive, a peculiar but undeniable aspect of commodity esthetics in the periphery.[12] This colonization is understood to proceed through relentless cultural bombardment, through the redundancy of its seductive messages. As the market framework interpenetrates with that of forms of life, the latter becomes reconstructed around their dependence on what was initially alien, using it for their practical adaptations, seeing themselves wholly or at least partially through it.

It would appear, however, that one can turn this sort of argument at least some of the way around. The form of life framework, as I have said, also has a redundancy of its own, built up through its ever recurrent daily activities, perhaps at least as strong as, or stronger than, any redundancy that the market framework can ever achieve. It may involve interpersonal relationships, resulting configurations of self and other, characteristic uses of symbolic modes.[13] There is perhaps a core here to which the market framework cannot reach, not even in the longer term, a core of culture which is not itself easily commoditized and to which the commodities of the market are not altogether relevant.

The inherent cultural power of the form of life framework could

---

[12] I have exemplified this in the Nigerian context in Ulf Hannerz, "Bush and Beento: Nigerian Popular Culture and the World." Paper presented in session on Transnational Practices and Representations of Modernity, Annual Meeting of the American Anthropological Association, Chicago, November 18–22, 1987.

[13] I am reminded here of Wolf's comment that what is referred to as "national character" is often lodged in such contexts and relationships. See Eric R. Wolf, "Kinship, Friendship and Patron-Client Relations in Complex Societies," in *The Social Anthropology of Complex Societies*, ed. Michael Banton (London: Travistock, 1966).

perhaps also be such that it colonizes the market framework, rather than vice versa. This is more in line with what I see as the maturation tendency; a notion which has its affinities with the peripheral corruption scenario, although probably with other evaluative overtones. The periphery, it is understood here, takes its time reshaping metropolitan culture to its own specifications. It is in phase one, so to speak, that the metropolitan forms in the periphery are most marked by their purity; but on closer scrutiny they turn out to stand there fairly ineffective, perhaps vulnerable, in their relative isolation. In a phase two, and in innumerable phases thereafter, as they are made to interact with whatever else exists in their new setting, there may be a mutual influence, but the metropolitan forms are somehow no longer so easily recognizable — they become hybridized. In these later phases, the terms of the cultural market for one thing are in a reasonable measure set from within the peripheral forms of life, as these have come to be constituted, highly variable of course in the degree to which they are themselves culturally defined in the terms drawn from the center.

Obviously what I have already said about the creativity of popular culture in much of the Third World, and not least in West Africa, fits in here. Local cultural entrepreneurs have gradually mastered the alien cultural forms which reach them through the transnational commodity flow and in other ways, taking them apart, tampering and tinkering with them in such a way that the resulting new forms are more responsive to, and at the same time in part outgrowths of, local everyday life.

In this connection I should return to the doubts I expressed before about the sense of time, or perhaps lacking sense of time, in the scenario of global homogenization. The onslaught of transnational influences, as often described or hinted at, seems just a bit too sudden. In West Africa, such influences have been filtering into the coastal societies for centuries already, although in earlier periods on a smaller scale and by modest means. There has been time to absorb the foreign influences, and to modify the modifications in turn and to fit shifting cultural forms to developing social structures, to situations and emerging audiences.[14] This, then, is the local scene which is

---

[14] For discussions of this in the context of West African popular music, see John M. Chernoff, "Africa Come Back: The Popular Music of West Africa," in

already in place to meet the transnational culture industries of the twentieth century. It is not a scene where the peripheral culture is utterly defenseless, but rather one where locally evolving alternatives to imports are available, and where there are people at hand to keep performing innovative acts of cultural brokerage.

The periphery in creolization

I should begin to pull things together. It is probably evident that I place some emphasis on the theme of maturation, and that I continue to resist the idea of saturation, at least in its unqualified form, which is that of global homogenization. In fact, in that form, it has suspiciously much in common with that 1940s or 1950s imagery of mass culture within the metropole which showed a faceless, undifferentiated crowd drowning in a flood of mediocre but mass-produced cultural commodities. Since then, metropolitan scholarship at home has mostly moved away from that imagery, toward much more subtle conceptions of the differentiation of publics, and the contextualized reception of culture industry products. Exporting the older, rather wornout and compromised notion to the periphery, consequently, looks suspiciously like another case of cultural dumping.[15]

It is no doubt a trifle unfortunate that there seems to be no single scenario to put in the place of that of global homogenization, with similarly strong — but more credible — claims to predictive power. But then prediction is not something the human sciences have been very good at, and in the case of the global ordering of culture, what I have said may at least contribute to some understanding of why this is so. The diversity of interlocking principles for the organization of cultural process involves too many uncertainties to allow us to say much that is very definite with regard to the aggregate outcome.

Repercussions: A Celebration of African-American Music, eds. Geoffrey Haydon and Dennis Marks (London: Century, 1985) and Christopher A. Waterman, "Asiko, Sakara and Palmwine: Popular Music and Social Identity in Inter-War Lagos," *Urban Anthropology,* 17 (1988):229–258.

[15] Cf. the critical discussion of media research in the 'cultural dependency' framework in J. O. Boyd-Barrett, "Cultural Dependency and the Mass Media," in *Culture, Society and the Media,* eds. Michael Gurevitch, Tony Bennett, James Curran and Janet Woollacott (London: Methuen, 1982).

A few points about how things seem to be going may at least sensitize to some issues in studying culture in the world, now and in the future. The center-periphery structure is one undeniable fact. When studying culture, we now have to think about the flow between places as well as that within them. Each society at the periphery, each Third World society, has its own cultural distinctiveness, but it is not as absolute as it has been (which was never quite absolute). Increasingly, distinctiveness is a matter of degree, as it has long been within that North Atlantic ecumene made up of a number of societies of the center and the semi-periphery; let us say between the United States, Germany, Sweden and Portugal. Interactions of many sorts have been going on in this ecumene over a very long time and the cultural affinities are obvious, yet nobody would deny that there are differences as well. Increasingly, however, we find the cultural differences within societies, rather than between them. If you look within some society for what is most uniquely distinctive, you will perhaps look among peasants rather than bank managers, in the country rather than in the city, among the old rather than the young. And obviously the reason is that through the operation of the varied frameworks for cultural process, and the interaction between them, some meanings and meaningful forms become much more localized, much more tied to space, than others. Using the word "societies" in the plural as we often do in a loose manner, conflating its meaning with that of "states," which refers to undeniably territorial phenomena, we are misled toward a very partial understanding of contemporary cultural process, as some of its frameworks are not contained within particular states.

If there is any term which has many of the right associations by which to describe the ongoing, historically cumulative cultural interrelatedness between center and periphery, it is, I think, "creolization," a borrowing from particular social and cultural histories by way of a more generalized linguistics.[16] I will not dwell on the potential of a creolization scenario for peripheral cultures very long

---

[16] I have discussed the idea of creolization in earlier publications. See Ulf Hannerz, "The World in Creolization," *Africa*, 57 (1987):546–59 and "American Culture: Creolized, Creolizing," in *American Culture: Creolized, Creolizing, and Other Lectures from the NAAS Biennial Conference in Uppsala*, May 28–31, 1987, ed. Erik Asard (Uppsala: Swedish Institute for North American Studies).

here, and it may be that what I take from a rather volatile field of linguistic thought is little more than a rough metaphor. Yet it has a number of components which are appropriate enough. I like it because it suggests that cultures, like languages, can be intrinsically of mixed origin, rather than historically pure and homogeneous. It clashes conspicuously, that is to say, with received assumptions about culture coming out of nineteenth century European nationalism. And the similarities between "creole" and "create" are not fortuitous. We have a sharper sense than usual that creole cultures result as people actively engage in making their own syntheses. With regard to the entire cultural inventory of humanity, creolization may involve losing some, but certainly gaining some, too. There is also in the creolization scenario the notion of a more or less open continuum, a gradation of living syntheses which can be seen to match the cultural distance between center and periphery. And just as it is understood to involve a political economy of language, so the creolization continuum can be seen in its organization of diversity to entail a political economy of culture.

Furthermore, there is the dimension of time. Looking backward, the creolist point of view recognizes history. Creole cultures are not instant products of the present but have had some time to develop and draw themselves together to at least some degree of coherence; generations have already been born into them, but have also kept working on them.[17] Looking forward, the creolization scenario is open-ended. This is perhaps an intellectual copout, but again, probably an inevitable one. It suggests that the saturation and maturation tendencies are not necessarily alternatives, but can appear in real life interwoven with one another. When the peripheral culture absorbs the influx of meanings and symbolic forms from the center and transforms them to make them in some considerable degree their own, they may at the same time so increase the cultural affinities between the center and the periphery that the passage of more cultural imports is facilitated. What the end state of all this will be is impossible to say, but it is possible that there is none.

Along the creolizing continuum, then, I see the various frameworks for cultural process exercising their continuous influence. Forms of

---

[17] Cf. Johannes Fabian, "Popular Culture in Africa: Findings and Conjectures," *Africa*, 48 (1978):315–334.

life, variously place-bound, take their positions on it, and help tie it together as the people involved also observe each other; the people in the small town idolizing the jet set, perhaps, and the jet set mythologizing the peasants. They may open themselves to varying degrees to the transnational cultural flow of the market, or allow middlemen to occupy the cultural space between the center and whatever is their place on the periphery. Or they may do both, since the two need not be mutually exclusive. Now and then a movement from the metropolis perhaps comes traveling along the continuum. At other times, what the metropolis offers may clash instead with a movement generated at the periphery. And finally, a word about the state. We have seen that the state is both a large-scale importer of culture from the center and a guardian of either more or less authentic traditions from the periphery. But in between, frequently, there is nothing, or not very much. Perhaps it is inevitable that the state, for the sake of its own legitimacy, is a promotor of uncreolized authenticity. Yet it is also possible that this is a rather quixotic struggle, a production of culture of dubious merit in the view of large parts of the citizenry whose minds are elsewhere. It may be a perverse proposal, but it could be that to play its part in cultural welfare, to cooperate with that citizenry in shaping intellectual and esthetic instruments which help people see where they are and who they are today, and decide where they want to go, the state has to be more self-consciously, but not self-deprecatingly, a participant in a mixed cultural economy, a creole state.

6. Interrogating Theories
of the Global

6. I. Going Beyond Global Babble

JANET ABU-LUGHOD

ONE CANNOT THINK OF A LARGER DOMAIN THAN GLOBAL NOR A broader topic than culture, especially if one wants also to understand (a) how *structural characteristics and politics* shape culture-creation and flows (as does Wallerstein), (b) the *processes* whereby such flows are unevenly articulated (as does Hannerz), or (c) the *form and content* of the new globalized culture (as does Robertson). The topic seems too big to handle. Even though I consider myself a macrosociologist, I felt uncomfortable with the high level of abstraction of much of the discourse I read in preparation for this session. The field, if not controlled, can degenerate into what we might call "global-babble." In many ways I was more comfortable with the approaches of Ulf Hannerz (and Stuart Hall, whose lectures I read later), since both try to capture the ambiguities and nuances of the concrete, as they are embedded in the lives of people.

That is what I should like to address, but I would like to expand Hannerz's approach to capture more of the cross-currents. His flow is still too one-way, from center to periphery; there is more movement from the periphery to the core than his exposition suggests (a point captured brilliantly by Stuart Hall). And had I more time, I would even argue that multiple cores are proliferating and some cultural power differences are actually decreasing. Only our own not-fully globalized perspective makes us blind to how the cultures of rising cores in Asia are diffusing within their own circuits.

How to get a handle on this gigantic and amorphous topic? Let me try to concretize via three cases.

First, in the traditional medieval city of Tunis, in a fashion very typical of an "Islamic" city, two suqs (linear bazaars) radiate from the great Zaytuniya Mosque which always constituted the geographic focal point and organizing principle of the old city. One suq leads from the mosque to the gateway that connects the medieval core to the French-built new city, and was once *the* suq. A second sets off at right angles to another exit from the formerly walled city. Over the years, a remarkable fissure has been developing in these suqs, which may provide a parable for the world.

The first suq now specializes in Tunisian handicrafts, "traditional" goods, etc. It has kept its exotic architecture and multicolored columnades. The plaintives sound of the ancient nose flute and the whining of Arabic music provide background for the European tourists in their shorts and T-shirts, who amble in twos and threes, stopping to look and to buy. Few natives, except for sellers, are to be seen. The second suq, formerly less important, is currently a bustling madhouse. It is packed with partially veiled women and younger Tunisian girls in blouses and skirts, with men in knee-length tunic/toga outfits or in a variety of pants and shirts, with children everywhere. Few foreigners can be seen. The background to the din is blaring rock and roll music, and piled high on the pushcarts that line the way are transistor radios, watches, blue jeans (some prewashed), rayon scarves, Lux face and Omo laundry soaps. Here is Hannerz's "market," the world of commodities. But note that, in the globalization of cultural artifacts that Hannerz describes, a two-way process of "objectification" is going on.

On the outskirts of the same city, men sit cross-legged on the floors of crude workshops, hand sewing the finishing touches on Gucci purses. In other sweatshops women sew seams on couturier creations. Here, without any doubt, is Wallerstein's international division of labor, with undeniable economic hegemony.

In the Census Office of the Tunisian government, where I had come to negotiate for access to census data (collected, following the advice of the United Nations, to make it uniform and comparable to the data of over 100 other nations) we discuss in French the mechanics of data transfer — IBM, Control Data, *sept piste* or *neuf piste*

(7 or 9 track tape). Here is the upper circuit of hi-tech/communication, fully globalized, but within the nation-state. Here is Robertson's global *Gesellschaft*. But only a few are privileged to it. I may have more in common with these Tunisian demographers than with my cleaning woman, but she has more in common with me than with a Tunisian domestic servant.

I present the second anecdote with a real cautionary. My eldest daughter, who is an anthropologist, lived for several years with a group of sedentarized bedouins in the western desert of Egypt. She recently returned for a visit. Stopping in Cairo, she learned that the newest, most popular singer in the country — his cassettes playing everywhere — was a young male bedouin rock singer whose music combines bedouin rhythms (actually, the "dancing horse" patterns) with western style music. Among the presents she took to the "tribe," then, were some of his cassettes, much appreciated by the young girls who found the singer's picture, on the cassette cover, "sexy." The older women commented that he looked "funny." There was clearly something wrong with his eyes (i.e., the older women didn't recognize his encoded sidelong glance as seductive). A proper man stares seriously ahead.

Now, this genre of mixed western and "oriental" music is proliferating all over the world. I was first introduced to it by a Belgian-American political scientist who fell in love with it in Germany, where Turkish migrant laborers had evolved a similar syncretic genre! I'm making a copy of my daughter's tape to pass on to the Belgian, who will probably send a copy to his German friends. From an ethnocentric point of view, what *we* tend to see is the westernization of oriental music, but I would like to propose an alternative diagnosis. What we are seeing is the orientalization of western music. As the early sociologists of American assimilation pointed out, it is a two-way street.

Thus far, my comments have been supportive of the convergence thesis. Granted, I see more movement from the periphery to the center than most people do. (Listen to popular music in the States these days and you'll pick up third world influences; walk down the streets of New York and you'll see third world culture imported and affecting Americans.) I do not deny the hegemonic influence of western patterns in the diffusion of the "nation state" (although *form* should never be confused with content, which varies widely), nor do I ignore the influence of central institutions, even that of otherwise impotent international organizations, in creating a western-based model of "modern" society with relatively uniform aspirations if not characteristics.

But culture is more than "traits," everyday practices, and even institutions — economic, educational, technological and political. The early anthropologists insisted it was, fundamentally, beliefs, "world views," and special constructions of reality. In the last analysis, that is what constitutes the hallmark of *civilizations*, in Wallerstein's view, or of true *globalization*, in Robertson's work. And here we seem a long way from convergence.

My third example, then, is drawn from the *Satanic Verses* — the author, the book, the reception, the battle lines that have been drawn about it. This case allows us to lay bare just what is syncretizing, what is globalizing, and what remains unconvergent in our so-called global village!

Let us employ Robertson's Weberian device of ideal types. A French historian (Chaunu) has used the term *univers cloisonnée* to describe the cultural condition of the globe before the formation of a western-hegemonic world system. While one can argue that there were more connections and linkages crossing the mosaic pieces of culturally distinctive regions than this term conveys (and I argue this in my book, *Before European Hegemony: The World System A.D. 1250–1350*), the basic point is well taken.

Now, in such a world, the recent *cause célèbre* could not have happened. Salman Rushdie would most probably have stayed where he was born — on the Indian subcontinent. He would have written in a language and genre of his region. And if he had written heresy, he would have been burned at the stake (as happened in Europe), impaled or halved at the waist (if in the Middle East), or met with whatever sad fate was traditional in his region. Furthermore, he would have been *aware* of what he was doing and the risk he was running — because he would have been addressing an audience of people within his piece of the mosaic. Moreover, he would have employed, albeit imaginatively and creatively, a *genre* of his culture. Thus, he would know that he communicated what he intended, and his readers would know what he meant by it. If indeed he were a renegade and an exile — and earlier world history contains not a few of these, individuals who left their original culture, adopted the ways of others, sometimes rose to prominence in their new cultures — he might have chosen to write a book, even a brutally sarcastic one, about his culture of origin. But in a cloissoneed universe, there is almost no way his work could have become known in the place he left. That did not happen. Nor did its opposite.

At the other extreme of globalization is an ideal type of instantaneous, indiscriminate and complete diffusion of all cultural products, with *no need for intermediate interpretation*. We are still very far from that. Rather, what we are experiencing is rapid, incomplete and highly differentiated flows in global transmission. We have a globalizing but not necessarily homogeneous culture. While in the last analysis, we think that this is good, enriching, and generative, we have not figured out how to live with the dilemmas it creates.

Clearly, we will need a lot of *verstehen* and will have to develop much more tolerance for the world views of others, no matter how offensive we find them. Communications have irretrievably shattered the cloissonéed character of cultural boundaries; there is no longer any place to hide. Wallerstein sees with radical vision the equally abhorrent choices — between a universalism based upon xenophobia and a globalization based upon a paralyzing cultural relativism. I think, however, that a third way is conceivable, at least romantically, namely: mutual awareness, sensitivity and, if not acceptance, an attempt to interpret and evaluate the beliefs and acts of others on their own, not our, terms. This need not lead to bland cultural relativism. It need not imply no values. One could still believe and prefer, one could choose to associate or disassociate, but one would have to learn to grant to *the other* his/her contextual wholeness. If we cannot go back to ignorance, we must move ahead to understanding.

Let us return to the Rushdie case. What, indeed, happened? I have been insisting to my arm-chair theorist friends that, before pontificating on the case, they read in full not only the *Satanic Verses* (rather than just the offensive excerpts) but some of his earlier works, especially *Midnight's Children*. For here is a satirist of rapier wit, for whom nothing is sacred — neither Mrs. Thatcher, whom he calls throughout Mrs. Torture; nor the anglophile Indian poseur (who in the novel turns into, or believes he has turned into, the devil); nor the Indian pop-movie star (who play gods so often that he becomes, or thinks he has become, the good angel, Gabriel, transmitting God's message to Mohammed); nor even the inviolate immutability of the Koran. (It reminds one of Post-Darwin discussions in the west about "who wrote the Bible" and of the so-called "monkey" trial.)

In the course of this James-Joycean-novel of puns and broadside hilarity, of dream sequences narrated conventionally and of bizarre "life" sequences narrated fantastically, one grasps immediately that the genre is pure post-modern West. In its intent as veiled social criticism, the novel descends linearly from Rabelais and Swift. Yet it uses the raw matter upon which all writers must draw — his own experiences, his own stream of consciousness associations, his own "culture," which, in this case, is Islamic and eastern, as well as British and cosmopolitan.

The audience it addresses — the English-speaking literati — recognizes the genre but not a large part of the "culture." The people who could understand the cultural content cannot recognize the genre.

As we have noted, in the *univers cloissonnée*, these two culture zones would have been buffered by distance and communication barriers. But today's global village offers few such protections. Rather, news of Rushdie's novel reaches Muslim bilinguals who perceive it as sacrilegeous — which it clearly is. They report this to their state officials, perhaps excerpting and translating the passages they find most offensive. The work is banned here and there (and not only in Muslim countries), is condemned, and finally, the head of an Islamic state condemns not just the book but the author. Inter alia, hundreds of Muslims in New York demonstrate in front of Barnes and Noble bookstore and in front of Viking publishers, whose office receives a bomb threat. (Up the street, fundamentalist Christians are picketing *The Last Temptation of Christ*.)

Nor is the response of western writers much more enlightened. Rallies are held and famous authors declare their fealty to freedom of expression. (Do they deplore western censorship? Do they notice it?) They passionately express their condemnation of Khomeini's "barbarism." Talk of trade retaliation surfaces. (So far, I haven't heard "Nuke 'em.") Virtually none of these authors has read the book. But even if they were to read it, will they ever be able to *understand* the response of a believing Muslim to this attack on a most fundamental tenet of the religion, the pristine God-givenness of the Koran, its immutability, and Mohammed as pure medium for its transmission? Can they be offended by an attack on what they don't believe?

This real event in such recent memory (Rushdie is still in hiding and the book is selling like hot-cakes) can stand as a very concrete instance of *how globalized* and yet *how unglobalized* CULTURE has become. How one analyzes what happened in *l'Affaire Rushdie*, and how one resolves the real conflict involved in it can give some hints about a deeper theory of global culture than we now have, and how, in grounded fashion, we should be looking for it.

6. II. Languages and Models
for Cultural Exchange

BARBARA ABOU-EL-HAJ

ULF HANNERZ HAS CHARACTERIZED AS ETHNOCENTRIC (I WOULD
say Eurocentric) current theorizations which conceive an emerging
global culture unfolding asymmetrically in homogenized or corrupt
forms generalized from west to east, from north to south. Eurocentric
is a relatively mild expression we apply to comparative studies
which fall short of their intentions because in fact they perpetuate old
regimes of thinking, continue into a hegemonic future the colonial
past and imperialist present. The predicted scenarios, for a homogenized or corrupt global culture, look like contemporary and decep-
tively milder versions of their colonial predecessor, the quasi-sci-
entific theory of vanishing races incapable of competing with European civilization, doomed to extinction, which justified efforts to assimilate or remove and finally to annihilate indigenous peoples. In their
modern forms and systematizing language, theories of homogenization and corruption offer their human subjects as little alternative to
massive subordination as was offered native Americans who, when
not killed outright, were "protected" by the Indian Removal Act of
1830.[1] An associated theory predicated the rise of the West upon the

---

[1] K. S. Hight, " 'Doomed to Perish': George Catlin's Depictions of the Man-

decline of the East, a "model of cultural study crystallized in the early colonial period, 1750-1850" for the Orient and very much alive among leading "orientalists."[2]

In place of homogenization and corruption, Hannerz offers a set of energizing variables: not global cultural production/ local reproduction, but reciprocity and synthesis, premised on the transforming nature of mutual cultural "flows." This formulation has a clear advantage in its capacity to decenter the powerful core-periphery formula which makes of world-systems in practice, if not in theory, a one-way penetration from center to margin, from strong to weak, from aggressive to passive and concentrates analytic energy on the global over the local. In the older practice culture is reflexive of unequal power relations operating in the sphere of ideology. Dominant culture is generated by groups whose concentration of power allows them to structure core and peripheral relations in favor of themselves and at the expense of those who are their economic, political and social objects. In the alternative suggested by Hannerz and argued by Immanuel Wallerstein, culture is an arena for struggle and transformation.

Yet reciprocity and synthesis seem also mild, suggest a capacity for equal exchanges in a world riddled with unequal exchanges. In Gramsci's terms, we might argue that the parameters of consensus, of hegemony, are never guaranteed, but profoundly volatile, charged from both directions in a tense exchange between manipulators and their intended objects, eloquently addressed by Stuart Hall in the opening essays. Yet, how are we to reconcile this volatility with the apparent power of cultural forms to serve so prodigiously the capacity of dominant groups to reproduce themselves on their own terms, to mobilize their vision into national and even global cultural norms?

The tendency to emphasize the center in cultural analyses is premised on the core-periphery model and its analyses of visible and profoundly unequal distribution of material and cultural power between centers where industrial and financial capital are concentrated and peripheries where they are not. In this model the remnants of

---

dan," *Art Journal* (Depictions of the Dispossessed, ed. C. F. Klein), 49 (1990):119-24.

[2] P. Gran, *Islamic Roots of Capitalism. Egypt, 1760-1840* (Austin: University of Texas Press, 1979) xi., and, of course, E. Said, *Orientalism* (New York: Penguin, 1978).

Eurocentrism lurk in the unequal attention given to the local stake in the reception and alliance with global power brokers, in strategies for a hierarchical distribution of power in local arenas marked as much by local class divisions as by international regimes of power.

Seemingly clear cases of local ambitions shaped by global interests can be profoundly local in their formation, for example nationalism, a European creation and a European import. Appeals to global political culture, in the form of nationalism and in the context of decolonization, served particularly well to consolidate for local elites positions of power vacated by the colonial predecessors with whom they were formerly allied. In these instances, locally-formed hierarchies were the essential condition for colonial and post-colonial regimes so often orchestrated by the same groups. From a western perspective, the cultural spheres of these political and economic processes in education, in shaping nationalizing histories, seem to epitomize a subordination of local to global culture. Perhaps the more significant pattern is the appropriation of global cultural forms because they suit so well the ambitions of local elites. Ulf Hannerz has described parallel agendas in peripheral states to "construct two (contradictory) cultures: the one of homogenization, as citizens with a coherent national identity; the other as differences, especially through education, to fit categories of individuals into different slots in the structure of production and reproduction," what Immanuel Wallerstein called dialectic and schizophrenia.

An instructive case of globally formed but locally produced historical culture can be observed in near Eastern historiography where Orientalist paradigms have been reproduced not only by those trained in Europe and the United States, but also in Middle Eastern universities. A generation of scholars, including Turks, has created modernist, and by definition secular, national histories predicated on the virtual exclusion of four to five hundred years of Ottoman history. Clearly these respond to global patterns, to the overwhelming historical paradigm of western imperialism: modernization theory. In this local form modernity is assimilated to the secular nation state. The Ottoman multi-ethnic, multi-regional empire is conceived only in its regressive, theocratic form, shaped by centuries of European fear and competition. Never is it conceived as a defeated alternative (transformed to be sure) to that European nation-state model whose current domination of local political systems appears inevitable only in retrospect, and in 1989–1990 increasingly transitional as a political

141

formation.[3]

Because the nation-state has been the political form under which international capital expanded, it does not follow that this political form and its cultural expression arise only from the center nor that it would have achieved its massive success without a corresponding local formation of merchant capital to receive global industrial and financial capital. Similarly cultural forms which help to shape capitalist social relations arise also in the periphery.[4] "The non-Western regions collaborating in the larger social transformation of the late eighteenth century had indigenous roots for their own modern capitalist cultures, formed through processes of indigenous struggle and in some form of struggle with the European part of the system. I am convinced that, properly understood, the industrial revolution was a global event, and I question the strong tradition in the West to assume a proprietary relationship to it."[5] In this formulation, class divisions occupy the center not the periphery and when we ask whose interests are served by the wholesale exclusion of a half millennium of Ottoman rule, we may answer perhaps the very same post-colonial architects of modern, Middle Eastern nation-states whose sources of power were formed indigenously and locally, in land and in merchant capital.

Who is central and who peripheral?

Our ambition to do equal justice to global and local is limited at the outset by our failure to generate a comparative language beyond the set of tidy binaries which reproduce the global regime in the very attempt to eviscerate it: center/periphery, core/periphery, western/non-western, developed/developing, etc. The periphery is, in Hannerz's phrase, "by no means a defense-less victim"; rather it has powerfully shaped the center, sweats from its pores. In truth the centers are somehow difficult to locate, to isolate. They are not concordant with national or even hemispheric boundaries. In the United

---

[3] R.A. Abou-El-Haj, "The Uses of the Past. Recent Arab Historiography of Ottoman Rule," *International Journal of Middle East Studies*, 14 (1982).

[4] Maxime Rodinson, *Islam and Capitalism*, Eng. trans. B. Pearce (New York: Penguin, 1973) 118-37.

[5] From Gran's introduction to his study of Egyptian cultural and material life, 1760-1840, p. xii.

States and United Kingdom, who indeed controls wealth? Between west and east, north and south, who are the debtors and who the debtees? Global capital works precisely across national frontiers, its boundaries formed by an international division of labor. In what relation does the underclass of New York City stand to that of Rio? The long progression of binary oppositions, divorced over time from their colonial and imperial roots, even when deprived of their spatial image, don't seem adequate to the task of providing descriptive or analytic power to fluid and volatile spheres of activity. If we cannot phrase an alternative, if an adequate language eludes us, how can we visualize a comparative theorization of culture(s)?

Global/local is a qualitative step forward. It suggests no charged hierarchical divisions, is less concordant with spatial boundaries or geographical regions, is capable of encompassing unequal distribution *within* as well as between national and regional entities. In Hannerz's formulation, cultures freely shape syntheses between the global and the local, "though always understood as themselves shaped by the international division of labor." Synthesis suggests reciprocal transformations, but abstractly, passively, and in this respect we may remain not too distant from the core-periphery model with its implicit treatment of the "third world" as receiver, overwhelmed by the authority, the sheer wealth of metropolitan culture distributed through the mass media apparatus of global technology. Hannerz resists this passive characterization as an "imaginary by-product of the awakening to global realities of many of us inhabitants of the center." So his scenario gives to local culture the capacity not only to take, but to give, to synthesize, to transform. How cultural transformations may shape material transformations receives little attention, although his "movements" category may be the space for this discussion. The "international division of labor" just begins to touch upon the horrific forms of subordination imposed by unequal exchanges, material, political, cultural. Sweat-shop labor in north Africa and east Los Angeles transgress spatial divisions.

To describe processes of cultural synthesis and transformation Hannerz offers "creolization," a "corrupt metaphor" now mainstreamed top down to describe a true cultural dialectic, its former racist baggage of debasement subverted. For those of us outside anthropological and sociological discourse, the after-image lingers uncomfortably. Beyond our primary categories, global/local, we have yet to find a language capable of describing equal exchange in a world of unequal exchanges. Is our vocabulary so impoverished because there is no such thing to be described, or because we have such difficulty envisaging it?

6. III. Specificity and Culture

MAUREEN TURIM

I BEGIN WITH A QUESTION: DOES CULTURAL HEGEMONY SIMPLY follow from, overlap with, and mimic economic and political domination? If so, then the study of culture would reveal an exceedingly simple narrative, an illustration of activities enacted in these other spheres alone. If the current economic moment is one of globalization, culture would simply follow that pattern, emanating from those areas which control the rest of the world. However, in studying culture, I find the situation far more complex. I am reminded of a passage in a particular cinematic text, Nagisa Oshima's *Merry Christmas, Mr. Lawrence* upon which I have worked, and its relationship to a source text, Lawrence Van Der Post's *The Sower and the Seed*. A character in the novel, Jack Celliers, is portrayed as thinking:

> He felt that the first necessity in life was to make the universal specific, the general particular, the collective individual and what was unconscious in us conscious.

This is a conclusion that Celliers arrives at after an emotionally devastating personal crisis. He is Afrikaans, attending a British-style boys' school where his hunchback younger brother is also enrolled. Due to the conformity exiged by this context, he fails to defend his deformed brother from harassment. This failure to act precipitates an unsettling of the self that permeates the rest of the novel.

While I don't subscribe to the oppositions offered in the quoted passage, I am struck by its will towards transformation, evidenced in the desire to make the universal specific. I cite it to raise basic questions about our patterns of logic, our ways of thinking. Are they dialectic? Do they move beyond the dialectic? Do they incorporate the specific and multiplicity that feminist criticism, particularly, has introduced into our discourse? These seem to be very important questions in this context, ones that call for anti-totalizing theories.

The models that have been dealt with by the essays in this volume are largely econocentric. The debate is over the form market imperative takes. It has not been on the role the market imperative has in the production and reception of culture.

One of the problems for me has been the absence of images, the absence of sound in addressing this throughout the conference. We have hermetically sealed our discourse off from the very objects and effects that we are meant to be considering. I want, therefore, in the rest of this intervention, to introduce some specific examples to begin a discussion of how the production of culture needs to be analyzed.

One comes from the Academy Awards presentation of 1989. The Academy Awards conjoin two industries, two parts of culture production, television and the film industry, that are increasingly intertwined. Moreover, this time, immense attention was devoted to the fact that the Academy Awards presentation itself was distributed by satellite and exhibited globally. It was continually discussed: this was on satellite and ninety-one countries were receiving it, either directly or by delay (at which point it would be translated). The spectators would be counted in the billions.

Early on, however, there was a disjuncture in the manner this text self-consciously signalled the global reception of culture. Comedienne Lily Tomlin came center stage after the first lavish and grotesque production number to joke about just this phenomenon, even as she presented it. She said, "Imagine the entire world trying to figure out what that meant." Her moment of irony, reflexivity and contradiction points out what we need to study in what we might call dominant global culture. We know culture is being produced for global consumption, but we don't know what the world makes of what it receives and we can not assume inherent meanings, whatever we might take those to mean. Culture is marked by a kind of polyvalence of meaning, a kind of multiplicity that is highly contextual and even internally confused. Knowing the site and means of production and the manner of distribution will not necessarily reveal how the texts of culture are consumed.

There is a lot more to say about the awards, not the least of which is to highlight the award to the National Film Board of Canada at the very moment that the U.S.-Canadian trade agreements threaten to annihilate remnants of a specifically Canadian culture. But the point is that the Academy Awards give us one way of looking at the American domination of culture in the world right now, a moment in which certain myths continue to circulate even if this process is filled with puzzling uncertainties.

A second example. Early in 1989, the French government presented a position paper in which the Minister of Culture, Jack Lang, responded to the fact that currently two thirds of the box office receipts in France were going to American films. Over French film history there have been governmental controls and even quotas on the importation of foreign films meant to stop this American domination; aiming only at the number of films screened, these controls can not address the way American films sell more tickets. Further attempts must be made to rescue the European film industry. We have to ask, if it is necessary to intervene to rescue the European film industry, what is going on in the rest of the world? Does this signal the end of French culture or German culture?

A look at a film like Wim Wender's *Paris, Texas* might lead us to say not yet. It was made by a German director with American money and distributed by American firms, but offers a European sensibility on an American subject. In terms of the dichotomy between financial investment and profit on one hand and notions of national identity and national discourses, you can have incredible splits. You can have America marketing Europe back to Europe. The same is true of every other country. We have a world system, but the lines of power and influence change direction depending on what aspect of production or reception are under scrutiny; the production of meanings continues to confuse. We can not simply assume we know the vectors shaped by articulations.

My third illustration: a short article in an advertising supplement to the *New York Times* (March 26, 1989) by a Japanese musician Riuichi Sakamoto. He argues that there are various trade imbalances, one to which he is subject. No one in America is buying foreign culture, while Japanese people buy American music all the time. Sakamoto is exaggerating and moreover his argument is being positioned ideologically in Japanese advertising against trade regulations; not only is his music well known in the U.S., but (to return to the Academy Awards) he won an Oscar for his score for *The Last Emperor* and became internationally known as the star of *Merry Christmas, Mr. Lawrence*. Yet there is something to his complaint; the culture industries in the United States are not suffering on the world market. They are amongst the most productive and rich industries that the U.S. have. Yet increasingly, they are owned by Japanese "parent" concerns or are dependent on Japanese investors.

As somebody who studies culture, the significance of these changes is all very apparent to me. Yet global economic models leave us almost bereft of a methodology for approaching the individual works themselves. Certainly, in looking at something like *Merry Christmas, Mr. Lawrence* we must consider that it is a film made for the global market. It's made with New Zealand and British money for international distribution. Its Japanese director couldn't find Japanese money willing to back him.

Yet the strategy of the film is to tell the enemy's story, in this case, the enemy from World War II, as embodied in the British and South African characters. It seeks to share in the manner in which they viewed the Japanese. This serves a debate about language, about the psyche and about identity, articulated around the trope of homosexuality and homosocial bonds. Two rock stars play the lead roles, Riuichi Sakamoto and David Bowie. This juxtaposition, this placement of contemporary stars into historical personas plays out with grand theatricality a conflict of identity and sexual attraction underlying absolute conflict. The Japanese command accuses Celliers (Bowie) of willfulness; his crime is assertion of the self. His crime is not his being the enemy, not his taking of British commands, but rather a willful disobedience at all points of command. Because of that, the film makes a very critical incursion into Japanese culture, where the projection of a self and a will remains culturally dangerous. Its readings elsewhere might be quite different; I have heard it read in the U.S. as Japanese cultural justification of their war effort because a British officer forgives his condemned former captor after the war.

Contradictory readings, unclear meanings, patterns of investment sometimes inverse to identities expressed and the nagging uncertainties of cultural reception — all combine to create a distortion to the map we might attempt to draw of our global culture. My examples, my arguments, are meant as questions.

6. IV. The Global, the Urban, and the World

WHAT CONTRIBUTIONS CAN THESE VARIOUS THEORIZATIONS OF "the world as a single place" make toward the understanding of contemporary cultural practices and of cultural transformations in the contemporary world? In attempting to answer this question, I want to address the topic of "culture, globalization and the world-system" in relation to three themes.

First, in regard to transformations in the built environment, in architecture, in the physical and spatial form of cities, and the meaning and significance of these changes, at a global scale; second, in relation to the views expressed in the principal papers here concerning the significance of the nation-state in the production of culture and the development of national cultures and identities. Finally, I want to make a few observations about the implications of globalization theory and the world-systems perspective for the study of cultural practice, and especially, the understanding of cultures on a global scale.

In the first instance, it would seem that a great deal might be learnt, and many of the abstract theorizations aired here could be operationalized and tested by studying certain aspects of the material world as they have been physically and spatially produced and expressed. Of course, this assumes that there *is* indeed an objective, "real" material world which exists independently of the discourses which are used to represent it. For people with an interest in architecture, in building and urban form, phrases used in our debates such as *constructions* of ethnicity, *concrete* cultural practices, ideas *grounded* in notions of the class subject, or discussions about the *erosion* or *rebuilding* of national identities, have an immediacy and physical referent which prompt me to start looking for their visual and spatial representation. Let me take some ideas from the many offered by the principal contributors to this symposium and illustrate more precisely what I mean.

Stuart Hall discusses at length the topic of "old and new identities" particularly with reference to England, though many of his insights are, of course, equally applicable elsewhere. This is especially the case in relation to the conditions creating the old collective social identities of class, region, gender, or race, as well as the "distinctive ethnic identity of Englishness." He also addressed the new conditions of international interdependence, national economic decline, international labor migration, and the "decline of the masculine gaze" which are contributing to these new identities.

Yet these transformations in subjectivity do not occur in a spatial vacuum, nor on an environmental *tabula rasa*. The old identities of class, region, gender, nation — of the whole place of Britain in the old, nineteenth century international division of labor — are massively and monumentally inscribed on the English landscape, in its cities, its politically produced house forms, its socially and culturally significant distinctions between "town" and "country" and the socially constructed terminology and mental images in which these not-so-subtle distinctions are written — "country house," "council estate," "tower block," "inner city." The material world constructs the mental and the mental, the material. Cultures are constituted in space and under specific economic and social conditions: they are physically and spatially as well as socially constructed, whether in regard to the economic basis of people's lives, the regions and places they inhabit, the degrees of segregation between them, the symbolic meanings of the world they create, the way they represent themselves through dwellings, or the visual markers they use to communicate meaning. These are all part of what Bourdieu refers to as the general *habitus*, a system of dispositions, a way of being.[1] Built

---

[1] Pierre Bourdieu, *Outline of a Theory of Practice* (Cambridge: Cambridge

environments and space are more than a "mere representation of social order" or a "mere environment" in which social relations and action takes place; physical and spatial form actually constitute as well as represent social and cultural existence: society is to a very large extent constituted through the buildings and spaces it creates.[2] In any discussion about identities, the built environment of space and place is a crucial, critical factor which both inhibits as well as facilitates the construction of new individual as well as social identities.

Or we may take one of the questions posed by Immanuel Wallerstein: how are boundaries drawn round specific cultures?

"Boundaries" are constantly being drawn round cultures, and sub-cultures, in terms of power, economic, political or social; territorial markers establish specific domains, whether laid down by the state, the market, by ethnic groups, or by people who are inside, or outside. Cultural insignia can be visual or spatial, static or carried around.

Third, we might take a suggestion made by Ulf Hannerz, that we lack sufficient scenarios for conceptualizing the processes of globalization. If we take globalization to refer to "the processes by which the world becomes a single place" or "the consciousness of the globe as such" then it should not be difficult to find examples of how the transnationalization of capital is changing the social organization of space and form on a global scale.[3] Roland Robertson has suggested that whilst concepts of the world or global economy are easy enough to demonstrate, notions of the world or global culture are less so. Yet in the nineteenth century, the gardens of the urban working class living in cramped rows of industrial housing in Britain were in the tea plantations of India or the sugar estates of the West Indies. This is a single space economy and a single cultural landscape, and needs to be examined as such.[4]

University Press, 1977) 214.

[2] L. Prior, "The architecture of the hospital: a study of spatial organization and medical knowledge," *British Journal of Sociology* 39 (1) (1988):86–113.

[3] See Anthony King, "Architecture, Capital and the Globalization of Culture," in *Global Culture. Nationalism, Globalization and Modernity*, ed. Mike Featherstone (London, Newbury Park, New Delhi: Sage, 1990):397–411.

[4] See "Buildings, architecture and the new international division of labor," in Anthony D. King, *Urbanism, Colonialism and the World-Economy* (London and New York: Routledge, 1990):130–149.

Elsewhere, Hannerz writes that, increasingly, we find cultural differences within societies rather than between them. I would take this further to suggest that if there is a "global culture" emerging it is the culture of contemporary post- (or even, in places, pre-) industrial capitalist urbanism; this may be what Stuart Hall calls "global mass culture" or rather, "global urbanity" characteristic of the contemporary world city. It is neither *trans*national nor *inter*national, each of which implies relations either between or across nations, but is global in Robertson's sense of "the world becoming a single place." Nor am I referring here to Wallerstein's elite who *believe* they live in a world culture. I refer rather to the culture, both material, social and symbolic, which enables an increasing number of scientists, academics, artists and other elites (and perhaps also a less privileged population) of widely different nationalities, languages, ethnicities and races to communicate more easily with each other than with others of their own ethnic or national background in the less globalized regions of their society. Of course, such a "global culture" could also be called another form of localism.

Let me turn to the subject of nationality and of national cultures and identities, all of which have been mentioned in the previous papers.

Two or three of the contributors have drawn attention to and even privileged the role of the state as the principal "organizer" of culture: it is also worth mentioning that while Hannerz notes a strengthening of national identity on the periphery, Hall points to its erosion at the core.

Yet if, as Wallerstein suggests, the nation-state is the main force behind "state organized culture," in the form of the whole apparatus of museums, educational systems, national archives, art galleries and the rest, why are these all so much alike? (This, of course, is a relative statement). What is it that accounts for their initial conception? There are clearly other powerful forces organizing "official" cultures apart from the nation-state, just as there are powerful forces organizing and influencing "unofficial" or "public cultures."

One insight into this question might be gained by examining the institutions and practices of what I would term the international (or is it global?) professional sub-cultures, of museology, of architecture, or urban planning and especially, the origin of their own, often unquestioned, supranational ideologies. In general terms, these have developed not simply in "the West" but under the very distinctive imperatives of a capitalist mode of production which has pre-empted global perceptions of "modernity." As Richard Handler has written:

> that most nation-states (and many "minority groups" as well) now seek to objectify unique cultures for themselves; that they import Western (including anthropological) definitions of what culture is; that they import Western technical routines to manage their objectified cultures; that they promote their "cultural self-image" internationally in an effort to woo the economically crucial tourist trade; that, in short, everyone wants to put (their) own culture in (their) own museums — all this indicates that modernity has not only conquered the world, but has ushered in a "postmodern" global society of objectified culture, pseudo-events and spectacles.[5]

Though what is problematic in Handler's comment here is his use of "modernity" to describe what, in the majority of cases, is the product of the capitalist world-economy. The extent to which states (or for that matter, towns and cities) do *not* have their own historical museums, do *not* have self-conscious "cultural policies," do *not* have "historically-informed" conservation policies and, if in the (sic) "non-Western" world, are *not* concerned about problems of "cultural homogenization," "national identity" and "Westernization," is the most accurate and telling comment on the uniqueness of their cultures and sub-cultures; the degree to which cultures are self-consciously "different" is an indication of how much they are the same.

Let me conclude by addressing what I see as some of the implications of "globalization" for the development of new theoretical models for studying cultural production on a global scale; for it would seem evident that globalization must make necessary totally new forms of knowledge in many different spheres. To do this, I want to return to Stuart Hall's story from Fanon's *Black Skins, White*

---

[5] Richard Handler, "Heritage and Hegemony: Recent works on historic preservation and interpretation," *Anthropological Quarterly*, 60 (1987):137–41. I am indebted to Larry McGinnis for this reference.

With regard to "global professionalism," the internationalization of the legal field under the conditions of contemporary capitalism is discussed by Yves Dezalay, "The *Big Bang* and the Law: The internationalization and restructuration of the legal field," in Featherstone, 279–94.

Masks, on the discovery of identity, and to quote Hall's comment: "the notion of two histories, one over here, one over there, never having spoken to one another, never having had anything to do with one another, is simply not tenable any longer in an increasingly globalized world."

If this means, on one hand, the whole unearthing of buried histories, it also means, on the other, the development of some kind of common conceptual language. It puts into question the entire set of labels, periodizations, categorizations which (generally in a totally Eurocentric way) "art," "architecture," and "cultural production" are generally discussed. Of course, it is naive to assume that histories and cultures which contest representations of each other on the basis of region, religion, gender, race, class, ethnicity or other criteria would ever have a common conceptual vocabulary, or agreed set of categorizations. Yet it does assume the existence of some kind of theoretical arena in which these contestations can take place. Current conceptualizations such as those offered by theories of globalization, the world-systems perspective, postmodernism, post-colonialism, post-imperialism (all, incidentally, coming out of "the West") are offered as this arena, though they are also, of course, in that arena themselves. Questions concerning the cultural effects of globalization, including the possibilities of a "global culture," may suggest to some that this marks the end point of a long debate; it is evident from the papers here that, on the contrary, it is rather the beginning.

6. V. Globalization, Totalization and the Discursive Field

JOHN TAGG

EVERYTHING BECAME DISCOURSE — PROVIDED WE CAN AGREE
on this word — that is to say, a system in which the central signified, the original or transcendental signified, is never absolutely present outside a system of differences.[1]

Jacques Derrida

I have been asked to say something about the proliferation of photographies in the context of this debate on "Culture, Globalization
and the World-System." The problem is that I have also been asked
to be brief and this may impose on what I want to say a certain negative tone: a refusal of a place in the debate and of its mode of
theorizing, without being able to go on to construct in detail the beginnings of other kinds of account. The difficulty is partly the present

---

[1] Jacques Derrida, *Writing and Difference*, trans. Alan Bass (Chicago: The
University of Chicago Press, 1978) 280.

context, not only this conference, but also the present state of the field of research which has hardly begun to provide adequate materials for extensive accounts of the world-wide dissemination of photography. It is, indeed, one of the great merits of today's debate that it directs our attention so forcefully to this need. And yet, I would still be resistant to the view that it is only empirical research that stands between us and a comprehensive account. Quite bluntly, I would suggest that the very desire for such an account is tied to notions of social totality and historiographical representation that are untenable. If we are to talk of global systems, then we shall have to ask whether concepts of globalization can be separated from theoretical totalizations.

Here, it would seem that I am in agreement with Roland Robertson that it would be difficult to see as anything but reductive and economistic Immanuel Wallerstein's injunction to work against the "very logical consequence" of "the process of masking the true existential situation," and "trace the actual development of the 'culture' . . . over time within the historical system which has given birth to this extensive and confusing use of the concept of culture, the modern world-system which is a capitalist world-economy."[2] Such "logic" seems to put us back, once more, in the primitive architecture of the base and superstructure model of the social whole. No matter how many staircases and landings are inserted, we still find ourselves trudging up and down the same metaphorical tenement, from the ground-floor shopfronts and workshops to the garrets in the roof, where the painters and photographers of bohème always have their studios. The communards have not yet pierced the walls and floors of this dwelling. The only difference seems to be that the local storefront now opens on a great global thoroughfare, beyond even Haussmann's imagination. The vista is expansive but, like Daguerre's diorama, its illusion of realism depends on our identifying with the imposed convention of its single, fixed perspective. As a representation of a social totality, it claims both too little and too much for what it wishes to see as a determinant space: evacuating from the "economic," cultural practices that have been increasingly structural to it, and collapsing the political effectivity of material modes of pro-

---

[2] Immanuel Wallerstein, "Culture as the Ideological Battleground of the Modern World-System," in *Global Culture: Nationalism, Globalization and Modernity*, ed. Mike Featherstone (London, Newbury Park and Delhi: Sage, 1991):35.

duction of meaning through a reflectionist concept of representation.

By contrast, I might agree with Roland Robertson that, far from being economically fixed and culturally masked, concepts of globalism have no status outside the fields of discourse and practice that constitute them. But here, too, I would have to depart from the way the construction of a range of representations of globality seems to be thought of by Robertson as the effect or expression of a real process of globalization, and even a "global-human condition," lying behind its "images" and knowable, somehow, outside the processes of representation.[3] Closely related to this is Robertson's claim for his own position that "globalization theory contains the seed of *an account as to why* there are current intellectual fashions of deconstruction, on the one hand, and postmodernist views concerning the 'confluence of everything with everything else', on the other."[4] For all his conviction that he is also opposed to "what poststructuralists and postmodernists now call a 'grand narrative',"[5] Robertson would still seem to be privileging some sort of master knowledge: a metatheory that can, like Wallerstein's or Jameson's reading of Marxism, account for all other types of theoretical production. For the so-called deconstructionists and postmodernists, one might reply that Robertson's notion of the world-as-a-single-place would seem to be caught in precisely what the Derridians might think of as a "metaphysics of presence," or the Lacanians as a projection onto the isolated image of the planet of an Imaginary wholeness that represses the multiple and heterogeneous positioning effects of language. Put briefly, the world that is systematic or one place can never be a world of discourse: this world is never present to itself; it never constitutes an accomplished totality.

Before I am indicted of idealism, let me begin to trace out something of what this might mean in relation to my designated "area" of photographies.[6] Perversely, perhaps, I can begin by conceding imme-

---

[3] Roland Robertson, "Globality, Global Culture and Images of World Order," in *Social Change and Modernity*, ed. Hans Haferkamp & Neil Smelser (Berkeley: University of California Press, 1991).

[4] Roland Robertson, "Globalization Theory and Civilizational Analysis," *Comparative Civilizations Review*, 17 (Fall 1987):22.

[5] Robertson, "Globality, Global Culture and Images of World Order," 4.

[6] For a more argued treatment of some of the themes sketched here, see: John Tagg, *The Burden of Representation, Essays on Photographies and Histories* (London: Macmillan, and Amherst: University of Massachusetts Press, 1988).

diately the importance of the perspectives opened by an understanding of the geographical expansion and increasing structural integration of capitalist production. This might have to be qualified to the extent that a neglect of specific local factors, such as national frameworks of patent and copyright law, would leave one unable to explain the different patterns of exploitation of the early daguerreotype and calotype processes or, indeed, the uneven constraints on the later development of national photographic and, subsequently, film industries. However, it is equally clear that a narrowly national focus would not allow one even to pose the question of the extraordinarily rapid proliferation of photographic practices in the nineteenth century, from the dissemination of daguerreotypes in the 1840s, through the entrepreneurial phase of mass produced portraiture, to the fully corporate stage of dry plate, camera and photofinishing industries of the 1880s and 90s.

It is also true that this latter development created crucial conditions not only for the vast expansion of the photographic economy, but also for the transformation of its institutional structures, in part as a reaction to the emergence of a broadly based, economically significant and aesthetically troubling sphere of amateur practice. To acknowledge this is not, however, to grant that we could ever derive the categories, constraints and motivations, or the cultural subordination, of amateur photographies from the technological and economic shifts themselves. To talk about the emergence of amateur photographies is to talk of the tracing out of new levels of meaning and practice, new hierarchies of cultural institutions, and new structures and codes of subjectivity: processes unquestionably bound up with technological innovation and the restructuring of production and marketing, but equally part of the momentum of a reconstitution of the family, sexuality, consumption and leisure that plots a new economy of desire and domination. And if we can follow this overdetermined development across a radiating cultural geography, it is never as a simple unrolling, economically and technologically driven process. The formation of amateur photographies had always to be negotiated in and across the fields of specific national structures, cultural conventions, languages, practices, constructed traditions and institutions. So far from expressing the necessity of a purely economic or even ideological process, amateur practices constituted a *discursive formation* in the fullest sense, saturated with relations of power, structuring new effects of pleasure, and generating new forms of subjectivity that have then to be seen as determinant conditions of capitalist growth in themselves.

We might take as another example the widespread emergence of instrumental photography, drawing on older practices of cartography and mechanical drawing and closely allied to the development of social statistics and specialized forms of writing. Its very function implied a universal and objective technique that would transcend the limits of all existing notational languages. Yet, for it to work, what had to be set in place were local discursive structures whose power and effectivity were never given in the technology, but had to be produced and negotiated across a constellation of new apparatuses that reconstituted the social as object of new disciplinary practices and technical discourses whose political character was elided. The institutionalization of record photography was not, therefore, just a matter of overcoming conservative resistance to a new technology, but a struggle over new languages and techniques and the agencies that claimed to control them. The notion of evidentiality, on which instrumental photographs depended, was not already and unproblematically in place: it had to be produced and institutionally sanctioned. And if, more generally, photography was taken to hold out the promise of an immediate and transparent means of representation, a universal and democratic language, and a tool for a universal science, then these claims, too, have to be treated as the specific, historical stakes of a politico-discursive struggle.

What I am arguing, against any totalizing or teleological view, is that the meaning and value of photographic practices cannot be adjudicated outside specific language games. Nor can a single range of technical devices guarantee the unity of the field of photographic meanings. A technology has no inherent value outside its mobilizations in specific discourses, practices, institutions and relations of power. Import and status have to be produced and effectively institutionalized and such institutionalizations do not describe a unified field or the working out of some essential causality. Even as they interlink in more or less extended chains, they are negotiated locally and discontinuously and are productive of value and meaning. And it is on this same ground that they would have to be challenged.

It is beyond my brief — and my time — to pursue the consequences of this discursive analysis for notions of a world or global culture. Returning to the models with which I began, I might, however, underline the following awkward points. In the first place, once one allows any effectivity to discursive practices in constituting

159

meaning and identity and generating effects of power, then there is
no longer any way of invoking another, determinant and exterior tier
of "social" explanation. But, beyond this, once one confronts the
openness and indeterminacy of the relational and differential logic of
the discursive field, then notions of social totality have to be radically
displaced. As Ernesto Laclau and Chantal Mouffe have argued:

> The incomplete character of every totality necessarily leads us to
> abandon, as a terrain of analysis, the premise of "society" as a
> sutured and self-defined totality. "Society" is not a valid object
> of discourse. There is no single underlying principle fixing —
> and hence constituting — the whole field of differences.[7]

If the "social" exists — and here we might usefully substitute the
"global" — it is only "as an effort to construct that impossible object,"[8] by a temporary and unstable domination of the field of dis-
cursivity, imposing a partial fixity that will be overflowed by the articulation of new differences. There is no end to this history. "Wholeness" cannot throw down its "crutches" and walk, restored.[9] We
have lost the guarantees of an immanent objective process, but that
very lack opens the way to the multiplication of forms of subversion
and the imagination of new identities, in which cultural strategies
can no longer be contained in a secondary role.

---

[7] Ernesto Laclau & Chantal Mouffe, *Hegemony and Socialist Strategy. Towards
a Radical Democratic Politics* (London, Verso, 1985) 111.

[8] Ibid., 112.

[9] See, Immanuel Wallerstein, "The Universal and the National. Can There Be
Such a Thing as a World Culture?" in this volume.

7. The Global and the Specific: Reconciling Conflicting Theories of Culture

JANET WOLFF

IT WAS A BRAVE AND FAR-SIGHTED VISION THAT COLLECTED SUCH disparate scholars and perspectives in the same symposium. Certainly, it was time that those interested in the global dimensions of culture met together and began the process of learning from one another the theoretical developments and growth in knowledge which relate to this issue. World-systems theory, already equipped to provide an account of the complex interconnectedness of the global system, particularly with regard to its economic and political dimensions, has recently begun to recognize the importance of culture in these processes. Globalization theories, which have generally privileged culture (or at least a specific notion of "culture"), seemed ready to benefit from a better understanding of the underlying social and material relations in which culture is produced (and which it, in turn, (re)produces). Anthropological theories of culture, rich in those empirical investigations which enable us to reject simplistic general theories, are well placed to combine ethnography with a more wide-ranging understanding of the relations of culture and society, center and periphery. And cultural theory, which includes recent developments in art, film and literary criticism, as well as cultural studies, has started to move away from its earlier rather ethnocentric approach, and to investigate the global dimensions of cultural production and consumption.[1] Here we had representatives of each of these traditions closeted together for a day, and willing to listen and to reconsider these issues from new points of view.

Two rather strange things occurred. In the first place, it appeared that there was general agreement among the three main speakers at the conference.[2] Varied though their contributions were, what was never at issue were the fundamentally different (and perhaps incompatible) theoretical positions on which they were based. Immanuel Wallerstein's Marxist perspective is obviously committed to the view that relations of production are primary in social process and social change. Although such a view can be modified to take account of the effectivity of culture (that is, it need not be a crude economic determinist model), it is not compatible with an approach, such as that of Roland Robertson, which *denies* the primacy of the economic.[3] Robertson's commitment is to a "voluntaristic world system theory"[4] which stresses the 'independent dynamics of global culture' (independent, that is, from polity and economy), and the cultural pluralism of the modern world system. His argument is that it is primarily consciousness *of* and response *to* globalization which affects and permeates the lives of people and societies.[5] This stress on the subjective, at odds with Wallerstein's perspective, also sits uneasily with Ulf Hannerz's more pragmatic analysis, with its focus on actual social

[1] See, for example, Malek Alloula, *The Colonial Harem* (Minneapolis: University of Minnesota Press, 1986); Pratibha Parmar, "Hateful Contraries: Media Images of Asian Women," *Ten 8*, no. 16, 1984. Reprinted in *Looking On. Images of Femininity in the Visual Arts and Media*, ed. Rosemary Betterton (London: Pandora Press, 1987); Homi K. Bhabha, "Signs Taken for Wonders: Questions of Ambivalence and Authority Under a Tree Outside Delhi, May 1817," in *'Race', Writing, and Difference*, ed. Henry Louis Gates, Jr. (Chicago: University of Chicago Press, 1986); Gayatri Chakravorty Spivak, "Can the Subaltern Speak?," in *Marxism and the Interpretation of Culture*, eds. Cary Nelson and Lawrence Grossberg (Urbana and Chicago: University of Illinois Press, 1988).
[2] Immanuel Wallerstein, Roland Robertson, Ulf Hannerz; Stuart Hall's lectures were delivered prior to the day of the symposium.
[3] Roland Robertson, "The Sociological Significance of Culture: Some General Considerations," *Theory, Culture and Society*, 5 (1988):20.
[4] Roland Robertson and Frank Lechner, "Modernization, Globalization and the Problem of Culture in World-Systems Theory," *Theory, Culture and Society*, 2 (1985):103.
[5] Robertson 1988, 22; Roland Robertson, "Globalization Theory and Civilizational Analysis," *Comparative Civilzations Review*, 17 (Fall 1987):23-4.

and economic processes at the periphery. On the other hand, Hannerz's conception of the operation of the economy (labour, commodities, markets) is different again, in theoretical orientation and in level of analysis, from that of Wallerstein.

Secondly, the real split in the day's proceedings occurred late in the afternoon, when it became clear that the discourse of those working in cultural theory[6] was of such a radically different order that the earlier proceedings had no way of transforming this particular debate (or, for that matter, vice versa). The ways in which art historians, film theorists and others explore the international dimensions of cultural production and dissemination seemed to have nothing in common with those other approaches.

The first of these phenomena was the one more in need of explanation. For what became increasingly clear to those listening to the papers delivered was the fact that there *was* no real debate. Indeed, despite the good intentions of the organizers and the contributors, we might conclude that such a dialogue is premature. In fact, there were far more serious divisions between the speakers than became apparent, in what was, for the most part, a polite, friendly and open-minded discussion.

Those who knew the work of the main speakers were probably expecting three major points of disagreement, none of which materialized. In the first place, we might have predicted an opposition between "economism" and "culturalism." This is an issue which Roland Robertson has already taken up with Immanuel Wallerstein.[7] Despite Wallerstein's attempt at this Symposium to take up questions of "culture," it is clear to me that nothing has changed in the very different points of view, and indeed conceptual frameworks, of these two writers. And yet this key question was absent from their debate.

Secondly, we might have expected an opposition between "grand sociological theory" and "concrete ethnography," knowing that the speakers were from different disciplines, and knowing, too, something about their style of work. Again, the opportunity was not taken up by either side to comment on the limitations of the other approach. Rather, the gentlemanly juxtaposition of papers suggested

---

[6] In particular John Tagg and Maureen Turim.

[7] See, for example, Robertson and Lechner, 1985.

(wrongly) that somehow these different approaches were different but compatible.

And thirdly, some knowledge of the different theoretical orientations of the speakers would have led us to expect an opposition between "systems theory" and "voluntarism," the latter emphasising action over structural constraint, and insisting on the role of motivated human behavior in effecting social change. This, too, is something which has been at issue in earlier publications.[8] And although many contemporary versions of Marxist theory eschew determinism and emphasize the constitutive role of human action, in the context of structural features of the social formation,[9] there is no doubt that the Marxism of world-systems theory is not (yet?) such a version. Nevertheless, there was silence on this issue at the symposium.

Despite the appearance of reconciliation and cooperation which characterized most of the day's proceedings, it was clear that little has changed in the main focus of the three main speakers. Roland Robertson is still primarily concerned with the *experience* of globalization and globality, and the ways in which this experience now pervades and affects social life throughout the world. (Indeed, "globality" in Robertson's analysis can almost be defined *as* consciousness of the world as one place, its existence — or, as we might say in an entirely different discourse, its "materiality" — consisting precisely in its centrality to human consciousness.) Immanuel Wallerstein, on the other hand, retains a central focus on the *reality* of the structures of the world system — those economic and political relations which constitute the interconnectedness of the contemporary world. Ulf Hannerz's main preoccupation is with the *processes* of cultural relations between different sectors and communities, and although he employs some of the vocabulary of world systems theory (particularly the notions of "center" and "periphery"), his work is different from Wallerstein's in its agnosticism on the question of primary structuring features of the world economy.

These differences, as I have said, were never articulated, either in the papers themselves or in the discussion among the speakers. In-

---

[8] Robertson, 1988.

[9] For example, Anthony Giddens, *Central Problems in Social Theory* (London: Macmillan, 1979); Veronica Beechey and James Donald, eds. *Subjectivity and Social Relations* (Milton Keynes/Philadelphia: Open University Press, 1985).

stead, we were left with the cosy impression that we were all addressing the same questions. In particular, the following appeared to be at issue:

— How useful is it to see contemporary societies as a world-system/in terms of globalization? (The different formulations, of course, disguise different perspectives, and imply accordingly different kinds of answer.)

— How extensive is this process of globalization? Has it led to an increasing, or even complete, homogeneity across social systems?

— What is the role of culture in the world-system/globalization process?

— What are the cultural relations between (and within) states in the context of the world-system/global system?

Consensus seemed to have been reached, implicitly where not explicitly, on a number of points:

— There is, indeed, a world-system (or, the world is a single, interconnected, place). There are important ways in which the world is interconnected, and it makes sense, therefore, to talk about globalization.

— However, we have to recognize the persistent (or, it sometimes seemed to be suggested, *consequent*[10]) diversity of cultures. That is, cultures continue to be diverse, and some of the ways in which they continue to be diverse are actually a product of increasing globalization, for example the extension of multi-national capital and of cultural products and media industries across the globe.

— Culture is of central importance to social and economic processes (though this importance is conceptualized very differently according to the particular theory of culture/society employed).

— We need an interdisciplinary approach to the study of culture in a global context.[11]

---

[10] See Ulf Hannerz in this volume; also "The World in Creolization," *Africa*, 57 (1987):546–559.

[11] This belief was not necessarily clearly stated at the symposium, but has been argued by each of the three main speakers. See Immanuel Wallerstein, "World-Systems Analysis," in *Social Theory Today*, eds. Anthony Giddens and Jonathon H. Turner (Cambridge: Polity Press, 1987); Robertson, 1988; Ulf Hannerz, "Theory in Anthropology: Small is Beautiful? The Problem of Complex Cultures," *Comparative Studies in Society and History*, 28 (1986):326–7.

So far, I have stressed the (unacknowledged) conflicts between the main speakers (and, we could add, between their work and the perspective and orientation of Stuart Hall's two lectures, with which each of the three speakers has serious differences). I want now to suggest that what they *share* is a failure to deal adequately with the question of culture in a global context. Ironically, given one of their agreed commitments, this failure results from an insufficiently interdisciplinary approach to the subject. For where they are all enthusiastic about the crossing of discipline boundaries within the social sciences, none of them has taken on the challenge of recent work in the humanities which provides a far more sophisticated analysis of cultural processes, texts and institutions.[12] This means that their theories and approaches remain unable to analyse cultural production and cultural texts. I shall identify five problematic areas here; what they have in common is an inability to take account of, first, *social process* and secondly *representation*.

[I] All three papers take as unproblematic such concepts as "West" and "Third World," "center" and "periphery," "metropolitan" and "local" cultures, as if the objects they described were coherent, identifiable entities. But each of these pairs is a *construct*, whose apparent identity is the product of a discourse and which (to switch to a somewhat different discourse myself) is ideologically imbued. We ought, therefore, to be taking these terms as problematic, and exploring how the terms, and our conceptions of those entities, have been constructed. The "dominant" term in each (West, center, metropolis, and so on), as Stuart Hall demonstrated in the first of his lectures, is defined in difference — constructed in opposition to the Other. It is not a monolithic, pre-existing, *real* subject, in any sense.

The "subordinate" term (Third World, periphery, local culture) is equally an invention, produced in a variety of post- and anti-colonial discourses (including Marxism, ethnography, theories of development). It posits or implies the existence of cultural and political sub-

---

[12] See, for example, Terry Eagleton, *Literary Theory. An Introduction* (Oxford: Blackwell, 1983); Constance Penley, ed., *Feminism and Film Theory* (London: Routledge, 1988); Richard Leppert and Susan McClary, eds., *Music and Society. The Politics and Composition, Performance and Reception* (Cambridge: Cambridge University Press, 1987); Tony Bennett et al., eds., *Culture, Ideology and Social Process* (Batsford, 1981).

166

jects, whose constitution and whose contradictory features are thereby obscured. Recent work in anthropology has shown that ethnographers, too, work with cultural constructs of the societies they study.[13] Rather than simply describing and presenting cultures, they *invent* them in a certain sense, through the discourses and models of their own investigation: they identify and label the group of the Other, attributing to it an essential identity which it does not possess.

An approach which took account of the discursive constitution of "cultures" — the ways in which they are *represented* — would already have access to the relations between cultures, here generally formulated simply as a problem to be addressed. For those cultures are constructed in relation to one another, produced, represented and perceived through the ideologies and narratives of situated discourses. This is not, of course, to deny the "reality" of relations of social and economic inequality between groups and between cultures. It is to insist that we do not make the mistake of granting these groups or cultures some "essential" existence, denying the linguistic and other strategies through which they are negotiated and produced. John Tagg's paper in this volume addresses this issue directly.

[2] All three of the main papers operate with an undifferentiated notion of "culture." It is true that Ulf Hannerz went to some trouble to itemize four "frameworks" of the cultural process (the market, the State, forms of life, and social movements), though it is not entirely clear whether these categories are intended to be exclusive, whether they are exhaustive, or whether they are equivalent (three different issues). Nevertheless, Hannerz shares with Robertson and Wallerstein a retention of a concept of "culture" which confuses a variety of processes, practices and levels of analysis. The authors often move without comment from one meaning to another; at other times they restrict themselves, also without comment, to one particular meaning. "Culture" therefore can mean: (i) ways of life (Hannerz); (ii) the arts and media (Hannerz; also Hall); (iii) political, or perhaps religious, culture (Wallerstein; also Hall); (iv) attitudes to globalization (Robertson).

---

[13] For an elaboration of this argument, see James Clifford, *The Predicament of Culture* (Cambridge, MA: Harvard University Press, 1988).

In fact, this loosely employed term describes a variety of different processes, institutions and discourses, whose separation and careful analysis is crucial to any discussion of culture in the global context. We need to look very carefully at the interrelations between these areas, and to examine the specific institutions, social processes, regimes of representation and so on, and their relationship to other "cultural" factors. This is a problem I return to at the end of my paper.

[3] All three of the main speakers ignore the level of the economic and the social. This might seem a peculiarly inappropriate comment to make about Immanuel Wallerstein, who has been criticized (by Robertson amongst others) for an *over*-emphasis on the economic. But in the paper presented to this conference, in his concern to pay due attention to the operations of "culture," he entirely by-passes questions of economic and material factors which pertain to cultural production and dissemination. His only references to a potentially materialist theory of culture (a theory for which I myself will argue) are of the order of stating that the capitalist world economy produces cultural diffusion. We need to know *how* this occurs. What are the primary economic structures which enable, contain and affect cultural production? In what circumstances does cultural resistance become possible? We need, as the contributions of John Tagg and Maureen Turim make clear, a way of investigating the nature and effects of the cultural industries, on a national and international level. We need to examine the role of technology, ownership, and cultural markets.

In other words, rather than simply situating a well-meaning discussion of "culture" within a pre-formulated model of international economic relations, we have to explore the *cultural* economic relations themselves.

By the same token, attention must be paid to the social processes involved in production of culture. An economism which gallantly switches its attentions to the operations of culture is still economism. Rather, it should undertake a radical reform of its assumptions, by acknowledging the *mediation* of the economic and the cultural through the level of the social. It must look, for example, at social class, relations of gender and of race, and at other social groups (sub-cultures, professional groups, and so on), and grasp the ways in which they mediate, through their practices, values and institutions, the production of culture. Culture is produced in a range of complex, and often contradictory, social processes. As Adorno pointed out fifty years ago in his critical comments to Walter Benjamin, culture is not simply the reflection or expression of the economic, but it is processed through social relations (and, we might add, systems of representation). Objecting to the simple connection Benjamin makes between themes in Baudelaire's work and economic features of the period (such as the duty on wine), Adorno urges that he recognize that the "materialist determination of cultural traits is only possible if it is mediated through the *total social process*."[14]

[4] Related to this last argument is the indifference of all three papers to the question of gender.[15] There are at least three reasons why we cannot discuss culture without discussing gender. In the first place, identity is always gendered identity. In his first paper, Stuart Hall demonstrated this very clearly, when he talked about the identity of the "English*man*" as precisely that. Political and other ideologies thus operate through notions of gender difference. This means that it is crucial to incorporate the feminist perspective into the discussion of culture and globalization. Discursive oppositions (West and non-West, self and Other, West and Orient, and so on) are also complexly interwoven with meanings and discourses of gender. As John Tagg emphasizes in his paper, cultural practices and institutions are also bound up with questions of family, sexuality and desire.

Secondly, we must recognize that the majority of studies of "third-world" cultures have described the experiences of men at the expense of those of women. As in every other intellectual and academic pursuit until recently, women have remained more or less invisible as a result of gender-biased investigations. Feminist anthropologists have begun to intervene in this field, though too often only by adding ethnographies of women to existing ethnographies of men (and thereby leaving unchallenged the very terms of a discipline which persists in finding the issue of gender irrelevant to its concerns). We might start here by taking seriously, and taking further, Ulf Hannerz's stress on divisions of labor, since such divisions are

---

[14] Theodor Adorno, "Letters to Walter Benjamin," in Ernst Bloch et al., *Aesthetics and Politics* (London: New Left Books, 1977):129.

[15] In the revised version of his paper, Roland Robertson does begin to address this issue.

always (amongst other things) gender-based.

Thirdly, the continuing failure across the social science disciplines to connect the public world of politics, economics, and institutions with the domestic sphere and with the sexual division of labor must be addressed in this context as within sociology generally. Just as the early development of industrial capitalism cannot be described purely in terms of production and profit, labor and capital, economics and politics, without widening our scope to grasp the location of these processes within relations of gender and the family, so contemporary relations of the world system must be perceived as unavoidably implicated in the sexual division of labour and in the practices and ideologies of the "separation of spheres." Feminist sociologists and historians have shown the inadequacy of our conception of the nineteenth century as a period in which there was an increasing division between the public and the private, the male and the female spheres, which were clearly demarcated.[16] Rather, the public and private spheres were interconnected, and interdependent, in many crucial respects. Women were still actively (if often indirectly) involved in their husbands' work. Family and marriage contacts were central to business and work procedures. Financial aspects of enterprise were often located in the domestic sphere (fathers-in-law lending money, for example). I am arguing here, then, that we must be prepared to investigate the interrelations of public and private, of the economy and the domestic, of male and female roles, and of ideologies of work and politics and ideologies of gender, in our attempt to theorize the global dimensions of culture and society.

[5] Finally, the papers are "pre-theoretical" with regard to developments in cultural theory. None of them is able to recognize the nature of culture as *representation*, nor its constitutive role with regard to ideology and social relations. They operate with a notion of "culture" as an identifiable realm or set of beliefs, objects and practices, more or less determined by social and economic relations, with more or less independence from and effectivity on the social process. Cultural theory, however, has stressed the "materiality" of culture, by which is meant the "determinacy and effectivity of signifying practic-

---

[16] See Leonore Davidoff and Catherine Hall, *Family Fortunes. Men and Women of the English Middle Class, 1780–1850* (London: Hutchinson, 1987).

es themselves."[17] Codes and conventions, narrative structures, and systems of representation in texts (literary, visual, filmic) produce meaning and inscribe ideological positions. In a rather extended sense of the word "material," then, they are perceived as having their own level of determinacy. Thus, work in literary studies and art history has analysed the *constitutive* nature of representation.[18]

This limitation in world-system and globalization theories in fact lies behind some of the earlier problems I have identified. The debate about "economism" thus takes place at the wrong level, and its resolution in the terms in which it is usually phrased still would not provide an adequate way of comprehending the relationship between culture and society. It is not, that is to say, a question of counterposing to a mechanistic, deterministic view (economism) a "better" account, stressing the "relative autonomy" of culture, or emphasizing the effects of culture in social change. Nor is it a question of investigating "cultural response" to economic factors. What is at issue here is the integral place of culture *in* social processes and in social change: the cultural formation and identity of social groups, as well as of ideologies, discourses, and practices. To take the example of gender, we have to recognize that women do not simply discover the reflection of their 'real' situation, or even the presentation of ideologies of that situation, in paintings, novels, religious tracts. Rather, it is in those very texts that ideologies are constructed, and that social relations are forged. The very codes of art and literature, the narrative structures of the text, are part of the ongoing process of the construction of meaning and, hence, of the social world.

These are the main difficulties confronted by the approaches taken by the three main papers. The authors are, as I have said, committed to crossing the boundaries between sociology, anthropology, and economic and political history. In suggesting that their problem is a *lack* of interdisciplinarity, I mean that an openness to other disciplines in the social sciences and, particularly, the humanities is a necessary

---

[17] Rosalind Coward, "Class, 'Culture' and the Social Formation," *Screen*, 18, 1 (1977):91.

[18] For example, Cora Kaplan, " 'Like a Housemaid's Fancies': The Representation of Working-Class Women in Nineteenth-Century Writing," in *Grafts. Feminist Cultural Criticism*, ed. Susan Sheridan (London: Verso, 1988). Lynda Nead, "The Magdalen in Modern Times: The Mythology of the Fallen Woman in Pre-Raphaelite Painting," in Betterton, 1987.

first step to addressing these difficulties, and it would also begin to bridge the gap between the concerns of these papers and those of the other speakers at the symposium. In particular, social history would illuminate the processes and social relations involved in identity formation; cultural theory would facilitate a grasp of the nature, complexity and operation of "culture;" and feminism would ensure a constant recognition of the centrality of questions of gender in any analysis of culture and society, at the national and international level.

The problem, in the end, is in connecting the title and the sub-title of the symposium (and of this volume). The hope of the organizers was that this connection could be made, and indeed, as I hope I have begun to show, such a development is essential and pressing. Leaving aside for the moment the matter of the particular theoretical implications of the terms "globalization" and "world-system," the fact is that we need a theory of culture at the level of the international, which is sensitive to the ways in which identity is constructed and represented in culture and in social relations. Stuart Hall's two papers indicate, in a preliminary way, how this might be accomplished. The three papers under discussion here, however, have focussed on the main title of the symposium, ignoring the challenges of the sub-title. Of course the very title and sub-title encode diverse discourses, which are only with difficulty reconciled, and it may be after all that the project of a dialogue is premature.

A central problem, increasingly apparent throughout the symposium, and already indicated at several points in this paper, is the definition of "culture." Roland Robertson has argued that his solution is not to define "culture," since the term has a complex history and is used in so many different ways.[19] But this clearly will not do. What *is* important is that we resist too narrow a definition of "culture," which would outlaw many of its other common uses. Rather, we must find a way of exploring the relationships between (for example), culture as values and beliefs, and culture as arts and media. Cultural studies and cultural theory offer the beginning of such an analysis, highlighting as they do the ways in which cultural texts participate in the construction of wider cultural values and ideologies. But this, in turn, must be linked with the sociological (and historical) analysis of institutions of cultural production (and cultural

---

[19] Robertson, 1988, 4.

172

reception): the necessary emphasis on the constitutive role of culture can otherwise too easily become a new idealism. Behind these cultural processes and institutions lie the social relations in which they exist (and which they also produce). And those social relations, as well as cultural texts and institutions, operate in the global context — a context, in turn, which consists of economic and material factors, social relations, and ideologies.

Building an adequate model of culture and representation in the global context will not be an easy matter. The proceedings of the symposium have at least made apparent what is now required: namely an account of culture in the contemporary world which grasps the fundamental economic factors in an international capitalist economy; which analyzes the cultural industries in this connection; which combines this with specific studies of local societies and their relationship to "cultural imperialism"; and which is based on an understanding of the complex relations of social formations, social and cultural processes and institutions, and the ideologies and systems of representation which create, maintain and subvert these.

Name Index

Urry, J., 73, 75
USA, 3, 6, 28, 99, 126, 141, 143, 148
  (See also America, North)
USSR, 99

Van der Post, L., 145
Vincent, T., 120

Wagar, W., 78, 88
Wall Street, 24
Wallerstein, I., xi, 2, 4, 10, 14,
  16, 18, 69, 74, 82, 91-105, 113,
  118, 131, 132, 134, 140, 141,
  151, 152, 156, 157, 160, 162,
  163, 164, 165, 167, 168

Washington, 24
Waterman, C. A., 125
Weber, M., 82, 83, 84
Wender, Wim, 147
Westminster, 108
Westphalia, Treaty of, 97
Williams, R., x, 3, 7, 46
Willis, P., 2, 3
Wolff, J., xi, xii, 1, 2, 3, 4, 12,
  13, 18, 161-73
Wolff, E., 123
Wollacott, J., 125
Wordsworth, W., 24

Zaytunia Mosque, 132

Subject Index

modernization theory, 141
modernization, x
movements, 115
multiculturalism, 55, 56, 79
multiculturality, 71, 87
museology, 152
museums, 153
music, 38, 94, 119, 120, 125, 132,
133, 147

nation-states, 4, 17, 20, 24, 25, 26,
27, 44, 62, 78, 87, 93, 96, 97, 99,
133, 141, 142, 152
national society, 9, 15
nationalism, 4, 16, 30, 33, 35, 69, 71,
78, 87, 92, 93, 96, 118, 127
new international information
order, 117
non-European, 72

objectification, 132
orientalists, 140
Ottoman history, 141

painting, ix
particularism, 71, 73, 74, 75, 76, 77,
78, 89, 103, 145
peace movement, 17, 115
perestroika, 89
"peripheral corruption", 108, 109,
124, 139
photography,-ies, 18, 37, 59, 155,
157, 158, 159
plantations, 48, 49, 115, 151
politics,-ical, 50, 51, 52, 57, 59, 61,
62, 63, 81, 100, 117, 150, 156, 169
polyethnicity, 71, 79, 86, 87
post-Fordist, 30
postcolonial,-ism, 3, 5, 6, 7, 9, 10,
13, 141, 142, 154, 166

postimperalism, 3, 7, 154
poststructuralists, 157
postmodernity,-ism, x, 8, 34, 36, 39,
71, 73, 74, 77, 136, 153, 154, 157
Protestant Ethic, 31
psychoanalysis, 47

race, ix, 7, 15, 60, 62, 150, 168
racism, 7, 14, 26, 55, 56
region, 17, 22, 150
relativism, 15, 73, 92, 135
religion,-s, 79, 83, 88, 92, 95, 101
relocalization, 12
renationalization, 12
representation, 14, 16, 20, 21, 28, 34,
35, 37, 49, 66, 67, 70, 73, 150, 151,
156, 159, 167, 173
"routinization of charisma", 101

school systems, 93, 97
sciences, 98
semiotics, 3
sexual division of labor, 30, 45
difference, 49
identity, 21
sexuality, 50, 158, 169
social science, 83
social theory, 82
socialism, 64, 74
societalism, 15, 87
societalization, 80
society, nationally-defined, 3, 10, 15
society,-ies, 79, 93, 126
sociology, 75, 82, 171
South Korean workers, 3
space, 116, 117, 150, 151
space, production of, 12
space economy, 151
state,-s, 17, 112, 113, 116, 126, 128
structuration theory, 86

technology, 93, 120, 133, 159
technoscapes, 10
television, 27, 87, 119, 120, 146
territory, 116, 118, 119, 126
Thatcherism, 23, 25, 26, 27, 31, 32, 66
Third World, 8, 13, 17, 23, 83, 110, 124, 126, 133, 143, 166
time, 127
totalizations, 156
town, 150
townscapes, 11
Turkish migrants, 3, 133

univers cloisonnée, 134
universal, 68, 91, 100
universalization, 69, 75, 77
universalism, 71, 73, 74, 75, 76, 78, 80, 89, 103, 145
urban design, ix
urban form, 150
urban planning, 152
urbanism, xi, 12, 18
Utilitarians, 83

Vietnamese community, 3
visual markers, 150

visual representation, 150
    texts, 171

war of positions, 57
West, the, 13, 15, 28, 33, 38, 39, 44, 46, 62, 83, 152, 154, 166, 169
Western episteme, 44
Westernization, 153
women, 26, 43, 58, 80, 81, 103, 111, 132, 133, 169, 170, 171
women's movement, 17, 115
working class, English, 4, 58, 151
world consciousness, 92
world cities, 18, 152
world economy, viii, 20, 98, 151, 153 (see also capitalist world economy)
world culture, 16, 91, 94, 98, 103, 111, 116
world, 11, 17
world-system,-s, ix, xi, xii, 1, 4, 9, 10, 11, 12, 70, 71, 74, 79, 82, 87, 92, 97, 98, 100, 114, 115, 118, 147, 149, 154, 156, 161, 162, 164, 172
worldism, 15, 73
writing, ix, 119

Notes on Contributors

Barbara Abou-El-Haj is associate professor of art history at Binghamton University, State University of New York. She is the author of *The Medieval Cult of Saints: Formations and Transformations* (Cambridge and New York: Cambridge University Press, 1994).

Janet Abu-Lughod is professor of sociology and director of REALM (Urban Research) Center on Lower Manhattan, New School for Social Research. Her most recent book is *The World System in the Thirteenth Century: Dead-End or Precursor?* (Washington, D.C.: American Historical Association, 1994).

Stuart Hall is professor of sociology at the Open University, UK. He was previously director of the Centre for Contemporary Cultural Studies at the University of Birmingham. His most recent book (with David Held and Tony McGrew) is *Modernity and Its Futures* (Cambridge: Polity, in association with the Open University, 1992). In 1989, Hall was Distinguished Visiting Scholar in Art History at the State University of New York at Binghamton.

Ulf Hannerz is professor and chair of the Department of Social Anthropology at the University of Stockholm and director of the research project "The World System of Culture" there. His most recent book is *Transnational Connections* (London and New York: Routledge, 1996).

Anthony D. King is professor of art history and of sociology at Binghamton University, State University of New York. He is the author of *Global Cities: Post-Imperialism and the Internationalisation of London* (London and New York: Routledge, 1990) and editor of *Re-Presenting the City: Ethnicity, Capital and Culture in the 21st-Century Metropolis* (London: Macmillan; New York: New York University Press, 1996).

Roland Robertson is professor of sociology and of religious studies at the University of Pittsburgh. He is the author of numerous books and papers on various aspects of the global situation, including *Globalization: Social Theory and Global Culture* (London, Newbury Park, and Delhi: Sage, 1992).

John Tagg is professor of art history at Binghamton University, State University of New York, and (1996–97) Fellow at the Society of Humanities, Cornell University. His most recent book is *Grounds of Dispute: Art History, Cultural Politics, and the Discursive Field* (London: Macmillan; Minneapolis: University of Minnesota Press, 1992).

Maureen Turim is professor of film studies and English at the University of Florida, Gainesville. Her most recent book is *Flashbacks in Film: History and Memory* (London and New York: Routledge, 1989).

Immanuel Wallerstein is Distinguished Professor of Sociology and director of the Fernand Braudel Center for the Study of Economies, Historical Systems, and Civilizations at Binghamton University, State University of New York. His most recent book is *After Liberalism* (New York: New Press, 1995).

Janet Wolff is professor of art history and director of the Visual and Cultural Studies Program at the University of Rochester. Her most recent book is *Resident Alien: Feminist Cultural Criticism* (Cambridge: Polity, 1995).